NIVERS SI D
INFC

Separate and Unequal

Discourse Approaches to Politics, Society and Culture

The series includes contributions that investigate political, social and cultural processes from a linguistic/discourse-analytic point of view. The aim is to publish monographs and edited volumes which combine language-based approaches with disciplines concerned essentially with human interaction — disciplines such as political science, international relations, social psychology, social anthropology, sociology, economics, and gender studies.

The book series complements the *Journal of Language and Politics*, edited by Ruth Wodak and Paul Chilton

General editors

Advisory board

Volume 3

Separate and Unequal: Judicial rhetoric and women's rights
by Huang Hoon Chng

Separate and Unequal

Judicial rhetoric and women's rights

Huang Hoon Chng
National University of Singapore

John Benjamins Publishing Company
Amsterdam / Philadelphia

∞™ The paper used in this publication meets the minimum requirements of American National Standard for Information Sciences – Permanence of Paper for Printed Library Materials, ANSI Z39.48-1984.

Library of Congress Cataloging-in-Publication Data

Chng, Huang Hoon
Separate and Unequal : Judicial rhetoric and women's rights / Huang Hoon Chng.
p. cm. (Discourse Approaches to Politics, Society and Culture, ISSN 1569-9463; v. 3)
Includes bibliographical references and index.
1. Women--Legal status, laws, etc.--United States--History. 2. Judicial process--United States--History. 3. Legal composition. 4. English language--Discourse analysis. I. Title. II. Series.

KF478 C49 2002
340'.14-dc21 2002066540
ISBN 90 272 2693 8 (Eur.) / 1 58811 214 4 (US) (Hb; alk. paper)

John Benjamins Publishing Co. · P.O. Box 36224 · 1020 ME Amsterdam · The Netherlands
John Benjamins North America · P.O. Box 27519 · Philadelphia PA 19118-0519 · USA

Contents

Acknowledgements

This is probably the most pleasant task to do in the long journey that brought about this book. I started thinking about gender in relation to law and linguistics in 1992 when I was a second semester graduate student pursuing my PhD at The University of Texas at Austin. The ideas that brewed in those years in graduate school finally took form in my dissertation, *Separate and Unequal: The Linguistic Legitimation of Ideology and Gender Relations in American Law (1995).* It has taken another 7 years to get these ideas presented in book form.

My heartfelt thanks are due to two fantastic teachers at UT-Austin—Professor Joel Sherzer and Professor Keith Walters. Joel and Keith are everything and more that one can ever wish for in teachers. I have benefited in so many ways from their incredible knowledge base and I have learnt more valuable lessons from them than I can count. More important to me however is their sense of commitment towards their students. I have indeed been privileged to have been a student of theirs.

John Benjamins Publishing Co. in Amsterdam has enabled me to convert my dissertation into the present book, and for this opportunity to publish with John Benjamins, I am extremely grateful. I have to thank my two editors, Professor Paul Chilton and Professor Ruth Wodak for their editorial input and feedback during the initial stages. I am also indebted to Paul for his meticulous editing and tireless effort in helping me make this book a little more readable in the later stages. Suffice it to say that he did not save on pencil lead in his effort to help me express my ideas more clearly. What remains unreadable cannot of course be attributed to him. At John Benjamins, I must thank Ms Bertie Kaal for her help every step of the way in the production of this book. Without Bertie, much of this cannot be achieved on time. I am sure there are many more at John Benjamins that an author does not get to know personally but who have nevertheless helped to make this possible—to all of them, thank you.

I am very grateful to Justice Ruth Bader Ginsburg who has shown me her support in many different ways. She has been a source of inspiration and she showed me in her own quiet ways how women can and must support one another in our quest for a better world. I also thank all my women friends who have given me their support at different times in my life. In particular, I must mention Sunita Abraham, Peggy Badlato, Wendy Bokhorst-Heng, Alice Chu,

Judith Clark, Vivienne Fong, Low Ee Ling, Virginia Maclovia, Anne Pakir, Chitra Sankaran, Maria Starz, Teng Su Ching, Helen Wilcox, and Yeo Soon Phek—all these women have given me that which is most valuable in this world—the gift of friendship. They have made the journey seem a lot shorter than it actually was.

Finally, I remain always thankful to my family whose love makes it all worthwhile. I dedicate this work to my mother, an amazing woman in so many of her unsung ways that only her children and grandchildren have the privilege to know.

Chng Huang Hoon
National University of Singapore
July 2002

Chapter 1

From past to present

Building on the foundation of ideas

1. Prologue

This book tells many stories, or if you prefer, this book tells a single story in many ways. First of all, this is a story about judicial discourse – the language of judges. Second, it is a story about gender discrimination and what the law has to say about it. And finally, it is concerned with issues of power and ideology, and how these propel the discourse of gender discrimination and individual rights. In such a complex tale, the ideas that are presented here are built upon a rich legacy of past and present scholarship. I will begin by giving a brief history of this scholarship, at once providing the context for this work, and also acknowledging an intellectual debt for which I am most grateful.

2. Building on the foundation of ideas: Of past lessons and present perspectives

> *Language is a guide to 'social reality.'* Though language is not ordinarily thought of as of essential interest to the students of social science, *it powerfully conditions all our thinking about social problems and processes.* Human beings do not live in the objective world alone, nor alone in the world of social activity as ordinarily understood, but are very much at the mercy of the particular language which has become the medium of expression for their society. It is quite an illusion to imagine that one adjusts to reality essentially without the use of language and that language is merely an incidental means of solving specific problems of communication or reflection. The fact of the matter is that the 'real world' is to a large extent unconsciously built up on the language habits of the group. No two languages are ever sufficiently similar to be considered as representing the same social reality. The worlds in which different societies live are distinct worlds, not merely the same world with different labels attached. . We see and hear and otherwise experience very largely as we do because the language habits of our community predispose certain choices of interpretation.
>
> Edward Sapir (1929: 68–69, italics added)

2.1 Language and worldview

In the *Tractatus Logico-Philosophicus* (1922), Ludwig Wittgenstein (1889–1951) set out to clarify the language-world relation in what is now popularly known as his 'picture theory' of meaning. Wittgenstein's opening assertion in the *Tractatus* defines 'the world' as "a totality of facts," not of things or objects, and he said of facts, which are expressed linguistically as "propositions", that they denote "states of affairs". In other words, the Wittgensteinian view of language, which is the totality of propositions, is that language describes 'the world' by picturing the states of affairs existing in the world. The Wittgensteinian dictum that "[t]he limits of my language mean the limits of my world" provides a clear idea of the extent to which he conceived of the language-world correspondence.

Another scholar who pondered deeply the language-world relationship is Edward Sapir (1884–1939), an American anthropologist. Viewing the issue from a linguistic and cultural viewpoint, Sapir (1929:68) characterized language as "a guide to 'social reality'" and asserted that it "powerfully conditions all our thinking about social problems and processes". Though W.V.O. Quine cautioned that the label or name of an object should never be mistaken for the thing itself (1961), I agree with Sapir that "it is generally difficult to make a complete divorce between objective reality and our linguistic symbols of reference to it" since "every experience, real or potential, is saturated with verbalism" (1933:11).

The 'Sapir-Whorf Hypothesis'[1] describes the language-worldview relationship in terms of the twin principles of linguistic determinism and linguistic relativity, which admit the same unmistakable link between the nature of language and the way speakers of particular languages view their world. Benjamin Lee Whorf (1897–1941) called language "the factor that limits free plasticity and rigidifies channels of development in the more autocratic way" (1941:156). In other words, language, or linguistic categories, affect(s) the way speakers of different languages, segment 'reality', thereby influencing, or some would even say determining, our view of 'the world' and our understanding of it.

The view of 'reality' as a linguistic and social construction adopted in this book arises from this Sapir-Whorf relativity. What this means is that speakers and writers employ language as an instrument to construct some preferred version of 'reality' along the lines of linguistic and cultural categories that are to some extent already inscribed in the language that is used. This kind of relativity acknowledges a certain degree of agency (thus paying heed to both the power of ideologies and the creativity of individuals), coupled with a small degree of determinism (to the extent that individuals are limited by linguistic categories and linguistically inscribed cultural prejudices). Particular constructions of 'reality' are thus closely associated with and constituted by particular languages and cultures.

Following the groundwork laid out by the Whorfian tradition, Dell Hymes' "ways of speaking" (1972b, 1973, 1974b) emphasize the idea that 'reality' is relative in the sense that how speakers view their world is in part constituted by particular styles of verbal interactions that are peculiar to their own speech community. As David Lee (1992:52) has pointed out, "it is the selective and idiosyncratic application of the resources of a language that plays the major role in the mediation of perspective". The emphasis on resources and the choices made by individuals signifies a very important shift in how scholars in the field increasingly think about the language-world issue today. I share this view of language: *language as a resource that individuals employ, rather than as a problem to be overcome.*

As the opening quote from Sapir shows, the constitutive nature of language is a well-recognized fact even in the early part of the 20th century. Forty years later, Dell Hymes acknowledged and reiterated the central role which language plays in human activities when he defines a "socially constituted linguistics" as being "concerned with 'social' as well as referential meaning, and with *language as part of communicative conduct and social action*" (1972b:316, italics added). In this characterization, we note the emphasis placed on the social nature of the linguistic system; i.e., that language is by its very nature a system that exists to serve a particular purpose in human interaction–communication. More importantly, Hymes takes Sapir's commitment one step further: while Sapir was contented with language as a "guide" to social reality, Hymes' emphasis is on *how language forms a central part of human action and conduct*. This view underlies the Hymesian perspective of a "socially constituted linguistics".

The task of a socially constituted linguistics is "the thoroughgoing critique of received notions and practices, from the standpoint of social meaning, that is, from a *functional* perspective" (Hymes 1972b:316; italics mine). Such a socially constituted linguistics is not only a crucial perspective to adopt in the study of language as a human and social institution, it is also a perspective that should guide researchers involved in any way with language issues for the simple reason that linguistic issues must be examined in the context of society and culture.

This book adopts a socially constituted approach, reflecting my endorsement of Hymes' commitment to "social relevance and social realism" (1972b: 317). Over and above the arbitrary associations between sound and meaning, there are motivated, social significances of the linguistic signs that permeate every single aspect of social life that we, as members of particular societies and cultures, cannot ignore. In other words, attention to linguistic signs must not be restricted to the purely referential, but must instead rise to the level of the social, the cultural, the ideological and the political. Or as Deborah Cameron puts it, language is a phenomenon that is "deeply implicated in culture, in society, in political relations at every level" (1990: 93). Hence, it is in the particular integration of Whorf's "fashions of speaking" (1941: 158) or, as Hymes calls them, the "ways of speaking" (1973: 73, 1974b) of situated individuals, that the significance of significations must be appreciated.

I am therefore committed to the idea that language is first and foremost a *human* institution and a *social* phenomenon. By emphasizing both the human and the social, I am reconstituting at the centre of the study of language the human faces in linguistic interactions, thus putting society back into language studies. As Hymes has said, privileging "human groups rather than grammar per se does not mean a neglect of careful linguistic analysis" (1972a: 37). What must be avoided is the alienation between language and society which constitutes a kind of "principled schizophrenia" (Hymes 1973: 60) that no scholar can afford to tolerate, for what is language without speakers, and what is society and culture without language?

In what may be read as a similar rejection of a homogeneous speech community, Mary Louise Pratt (1987) adopts Benedict Anderson's concept of "imagined communities" (1983), and asserts that "nobody's world will be found to be linguistically or subjectively homogeneous, not even that of dominant classes. When seen as a site of social reproduction and struggle, language cannot be imagined as unified" (p.62). In short, whatever the imagined speech community in linguistic research may be, it must be *a speech community consisting of actual speakers who engage constantly in living discourses of contest and consent. The speech community is therefore always heterogeneous, always emerging, and always teeming with variation.*

Hymes has also noted that "we have no general perspective on *language as a human problem*, not even an integrated body of works in search of one" (1973:60, italics mine). The "human problem" alluded to is the important question of linguistic inequality, which Hymes identifies as "the origins and foundations of inequality among speakers" (1973). Since Hymes, William Labov has spoken up on the issue of linguistic (and hence, social) inequality. In his works, Labov has argued both for "the logic of nonstandard English" (1970) and also called for "objectivity and commitment" in linguistic research, especially when one deals with particularly sensitive issues (such as, the problems faced by African-Americans in education) (Labov 1982).

More recently, the work on "standard language ideology"[2] by Lippi-Green (1994, 1997) continues the tradition of identifying linguistic issues with problems of discrimination. Standard language ideology is defined as "a bias toward an abstracted, idealized, homogeneous spoken language which is imposed from above, and which takes as its model the written language. The most salient feature is the goal of suppression of variation of all kinds" (Lippi-Green 1994:166). Lippi-Green discusses the ways in which education and the media are means by which this dominant ideology is maintained and then used to discriminate against 'detractors' from this preferred and legitimated linguistic norm. Like linguistic prescriptivism (Kroch and Small 1978; Milroy and Milroy 1985), the imposition of an educated norm when taken to extremes results in serious discrimination of those who are perceived to have the 'wrong' accent or the 'lesser' variety.

This book aims to contribute in a similar spirit to promote awareness of existing inequalities in a very specialized context – the judicial context – through a critical examination of judicial discourse. By stressing the humanity in language studies and the socio-cultural and political basis of linguistic usage, I seek to promote an understanding of the law and law's power via a study of judicial opinions, so as to work towards social equality via a critique of linguistically constructed legal inequalities.

Though I do not want to go so far as to endorse the strong version of linguistic determinism, it remains a fact that language plays a significantly constitutive role in defining human social relations. James Boyd White, a literary critic and legal scholar argues that (1984:21, emphasis added):

> *whenever we speak or write, whether we know it or not and for good or ill, we contribute to the creation of a culture*, and we do so both in the way we reconstitute

> our language and in the relation we establish with the other person who is our reader. Every way of reading is a way of being and acting in the world.

Language is thus both the medium and the means individuals employ to construct their own social realities in their daily discourses. By viewing speaking, reading and writing as a linguistic and social act in the construction of worldviews, we recall once again the insights of J.L. Austin (1962) and Roman Jakobson (1990), among others, who taught us that language is primarily a social activity in which individuals learn, literally, how to do things with their words. It is thus through the language we use, i.e., through our daily discourses, that we constitute and reconstitute our socio-political and cultural realities, vying constantly for the right to control and to define a particular worldview that is consistent with one's own ideology. These constant contestations for the right to define and control 'reality' (socio-cultural, political, etc) through linguistic constructions and discursive interventions directly contribute to the idea of linguistic and cultural relativity, and it is this relativism that motivates a critical and more vigilant perspective towards the study of discourse.

George Lakoff and Mark Johnson (1980) underscore the same point by showing that the metaphors which are commonly invoked in everyday discourse reveal in an important way the nature and structure of our world. Norman Fairclough (1992: 194, emphasis added) agrees with them on this issue:

> Metaphors are pervasive in all sorts of language and in all sorts of discourse. . *When we signify things through one metaphor rather than another, we are constructing our reality in one way rather than another.* Metaphors structure the way we think and the way we act, and our systems of knowledge and belief, in a pervasive and fundamental way.

Contrary to the old view of perceiving the language-world relationship in terms of a somewhat (in retrospect) simplistic referential or correspondence theory of matching objects 'out there' in 'the world' with their 'properly' given names or labels, scholars have recently revolutionized their entire thought orientation. In short, scholars working within the construction view have rejected both the classical view of language as a mirror on 'the world' and the objectivist metaphysics which accompanies the view, the result of which is that the construction paradigm, which is the perspective adopted here, gives a more central and dynamic role to language. Language, in a nutshell, does not merely consist of labels for everything in 'the world'. Recall once again Sapir's statement, for example, that: "The worlds in which different societies live are distinct worlds, not merely the same world with different labels attached".

Language thus plays a constitutive role, not viewed as a means to lamely describe or to reflect 'the way the world is,' but as actively constructing and defining 'the world' as it is used in social dialogue. In our discursive practices then, we build up our particular worldview as we participate in linguistic interactions during social encounters. Simply stated, "language does not reflect culture but . . *language use in discourse creates, recreates, and modifies culture*" (Sherzer 1987: 300, italics added). This way of conceptualizing language as a dynamic and ever-evolving form of social practice, and of viewing language as having a central and critical role to play in structuring verbal interactions will prove more productive in the long run.

2.2 Language and ideology

A socially constituted linguistics, given that it seeks to understand life as it is lived through discourse, must be a *critical* enterprise. Thus, discursive practices are viewed here not only in terms of *how* individuals interact or *what* is being conveyed, but also in terms of *why* individuals do what they do. The kinds of ideologies that guide individual (discursive) acts are central concerns to be explored in this book. In short, I will engage in *an interrogation of discursive practices* in the spirit of critical linguistics (Fowler et al. 1979), a tradition that emphasizes the role of ideology.

The assumption about language and 'reality' adopted here has been nicely characterized by Duranti (1994: 4–5) when he writes:

> reality is routinely negotiated by participants in an interaction and that "facts" are constituted differently according to the points of view of the actors involved, the norms evoked, and the processes activated within specific institutional settings (e.g., legal, medical, educational). This view does not imply that there is no reality outside of talk or that all interpretations are equally acceptable, but rather it holds that in institutional as well as in mundane settings various versions of reality are proposed, sustained, or challenged precisely by the language that describes and sustains them and that such negotiations are not irrelevant linguistic games but potentially important social acts.

To this end, there is now an increasing emphasis on 'discourse' as a legitimate level of analysis (witness for example both Greg Urban's and Joel Sherzer's "discourse-centered approach" to language and culture; Fairclough's "textually-oriented discourse analysis"; and the text-based discourse analysis that comprises the bulk of this work).

Consistent with the construction view of language use is a series of critical practices that have emerged across different disciplines. In linguistics, for instance, the works of Roger Fowler and his associates have revolved around the rejection of the classical idea that language objectively reflects our world (Fowler et al. 1979). Classical analyses are said to have failed to take into account the purpose-driven nature of language use as situated within a specific local and/or global socio-cultural and ideological-political economy. Critical linguists, such as the East Anglian researchers, adopt the view that "all linguistic usage encodes ideological patterns or discursive structures which mediate representations of the world in language" (Fowler 1991:89). Thus, language is far from being an ancillary, accidental factor in any social context in which it happens to find itself, but is instead a kind of *purposive* instrument which users actively wield "to explore, systematize, transform, and often obscure, analyses of reality; to regulate the ideas and behaviour of others; to classify and rank people, events and objects; to assert institutional or personal status" (Fowler et al. 1979:3). The overtly Whorfian overtone is unmistakable: *language and language use are not neutral enterprises.*

The basic tenets of critical linguistics are that language use is influenced by ideological motivations and that choices are made in the context of economic, political and ideological realities (1979). Fowler et al. also sought through a critical analysis of written texts to unveil the "linguistic processes which are instruments in social inequality and the concealment of truth" (p.2). In these statements, the place in which ideology is embedded is clearly evident: ideological motivations are the propellers and determinants in the shaping of texts and the structuring of discourse. This view of ideology as deeply implicated in linguistic usage remains fairly constant in later works in critical linguistics.

Joel Sherzer's (1993) review of Lee (1992) highlights the fact that Lee and other critical linguists focus primarily on "the centrality of conflicting ideologies in the study of language" (Sherzer 1993:275). Sherzer questions critical linguists for "always trying to find political and ideological consequences of language use" (p.c.). Though Sherzer's point is well taken, my view is that it is not so much that critical linguists insist on focusing only on the political and ideological aspects, but that a critical approach to linguistic analysis is distinguished from other approaches by its heightened awareness of ideological prejudices influencing language use. Furthermore the political and the ideological need not always suggest something that is negative (as Michel Foucault had also emphasized); instead the emphasis is on the *purposive* nature of linguistic exchanges.

Paul Friedrich's "linguacultural ideology" (1989) recognizes that language and culture "constitute *a single universe* of its own kind, the part of which are bound at least as much to each other as to anything else outside that universe" (p.306, italics added). This emphasis on the unity of the linguistic and the cultural is a soundly directed mode of thinking because it acknowledges the constitutive nature of language in the production and reproduction of sociocultural meanings. Friedrich also underscores the power of linguacultural ideology: that it is "more diffuse, pervasive, and comprehensive" than other kinds of ideology, but yet it is paradoxically "more located in the unconscious or subconscious of the speaker and speaker collectivities" than any other type of ideology that may be also present (p.307). In other words, linguacultural ideology is powerful because it is simultaneously nowhere and everywhere, i.e., that it is not localized, and its power derives from the fact that it is inscribed in language. The concept of 'linguacultural ideology' is therefore especially useful for scholars, and I include myself here, who are concerned with how language, culture and ideology intersect.

Michael Silverstein, working from a rather different perspective, made similar links between "language structure and linguistic ideology" (1979). Building upon the views of Boas, Sapir and Whorf, Silverstein made the leap by "refocus[ing] Whorf's 'habitual thought and behavior' as 'ideology'" (Hill and Mannheim 1992: 395). Linguistic ideologies are "any sets of beliefs about language articulated by the users as a rationalization or justification of perceived language structure and use" (Silverstein 1979: 193). Silverstein's work thus takes us beyond the plane of semantic reference into a pragmatic and semiotic theory of indexical relations couched at the intersection of structure, usage and ideology (1979, 1985). The process of ideological rationalization is expressed within "the paradigm of interested human social action" and the "conscious purposivity in language use" (Silverstein 1985: 222–223).

Addressing the problems faced by the American working-class in its confrontation with the law, Merry combines the anthropological view of ideology with the Marxist view of ideology. She argues that (1986: 253–254, emphasis added):

> *Thinking of ideology as culture highlights questions of harmony, integration, and consensus, while thinking of ideology in terms of power and dominance highlights questions of conflict, control, and hegemony.*

Merry's conception of ideology as a double-faceted motivating force is more satisfying than the view of ideology as rationalization, justification or a kind of concealment of 'the truth'; it is in fact reminiscent of both Michel Foucault's rejection of ideology as a highly problematic notion (1972–1977: 118) and Pierre Bourdieu's idea of symbolic power and domination (1977: 163ff.).

Foucault rejected the notion of ideology precisely for the reasons that there is no absolute truth or falsity that ideology is suggested to be opposed to, and that 'ideology' hints at a tangible, agentive subject when the propeller behind any action is, at its base, discursive in nature. Furthermore, ideology is seen to exist apart from and secondary to the social and political infrastructure when the 'truth' is that all these structures are part and parcel of a social process that is linguistically engendered.

Bourdieu, on the other hand, speaks of ideology as simultaneously "doubly determined" (1977: 169) by the dominating class and the subjugated masses. Power resides in the use and control of the terms of a "legitimate language" (1982a: 43ff.) employed to perpetuate a specific ideology of the ruling class and at the same time exploited to keep the subjugated masses from grasping the basis for their enslavement. This is the essence of symbolic domination: an insidious employment and deployment of power that is at once real but yet not tangible, where the effects of power and ideology are felt and lived but not apprehended. Merry's definition is thus an appreciation and acceptance of the Janus-like nature of ideology as a powerful force yielding both positive and negative effects. I shall be employing this conception here.

Mary Louise Pratt (1982) alerts us to the nature of "conventions of representation" of reality, or points of view. Pratt demonstrated through an examination of a series of literary texts and travel tales that the textual deployment of generic conventions of representing the world requires that we read these texts with an awareness of what these pre-selected perspectives mean for the author and the effects these choices exerted on the readership. Pratt's analysis, therefore, brought together the aesthetic and the socio-ideological dimensions of text production. While Pratt's conception of how ideology comes into play in textual structuring is by now not new, what is instructive about Pratt's work is the reflexivity in which she brought into her own research. She has this important reminder for scholars who work in the same mode (1982: 154):

> The foregoing discussion [i.e., her own analysis] will doubtless have communicated a set of ideological commitments of my own – a criticism of discourses that implicitly or explicitly dehumanize, trivialize, and devalue other realities in the name of Western superiority, and an appreciation of discourses that do not do these things, and instead acknowledge the limitations on the West's ability to make sense of other peoples and places (especially those it seeks to hold in subjugation). Some may wish to argue that such commitments have no place in academic investigations, or in linguistics, but I think they are wrong. To begin with, that argument is obviously as ideologically committed as my own. More generally, any discourse has ideological dimensions – values – just as it has esthetic and sociological ones. Poetics and sociolinguistics are equipping us with a stylistics that can deal with these latter two dimensions. Ultimately, we will need a stylistics that can deal with the first one too.

The central claim made here is that *language use is a motivated act* that betrays one's socio-cultural identity and one's ideology, and that "the failure to acknowledge ideology creates the illusion of an objective, 'pure' sphere of enquiry" (Joseph 1990: 52). When users engage in linguistic interactions of any sort, what users are in fact doing, or are seeking to achieve, is *the control of a particular version of 'reality' through discursive negotiations*. This desire for controlling the representation of a specific worldview is guided by either personal or institutional ideology, or both, acting within each individual. Dominant ideology is thus defined, "not as a neutral system of ideas but rather as the way in which meaning, and thus language, seems to sustain relations of domination" (Gal 1989: 359). Locating ideology in language use is an important dimension in the construction view of language since it brings into focus the idea of power and power struggles at the site of discursive practices. Or as Teun A.van Dijk (1998: 6) has put it, quite simply, "if we want to know what ideologies actually look like, how they work, and how they are created, changed and reproduced, we need to look closely at their discursive manifestations".

The work of Susan Gal (1989, 1991) on political economy and resistance discourse draws our attention to several important issues. First, language use is situated more globally in the context of a political economy. With the introduction of a political economy, Gal has effectively linked linguistic interactions not just to the immediate social and cultural context, but also to the nature of the wider infra-structural set-up, which means that institutional ideology and values are also directly implicated. Second, Gal also alerts us to the need to pay attention to the silences and gaps in discourse, whether spoken or written. Silence is traditionally seen as a crippling feature in discourse –

what is not said or expressed is somehow unimportant, powerless and insignificant. What Gal has done is to direct attention to "the paradoxical power of silence" (1991: 175). In this context, Gal is right to caution us about the selectivity that is inherent even in ethnographic studies, which aspire to the ideal of a local and global contextualization in researching and interpreting other cultures. Gal (1991: 190, emphasis added) writes,

> [b]y claiming to accurately represent the facts about an exotic culture, the naive realist conventions of ethnographic writing implicitly deny that *ethnographic facts are selected, indeed constructed,* in the encounter between the anthropologist and the 'other' who is her/his subject.

Gal also argued against Bourdieu's view of symbolic domination as ignoring a crucial fact that 'mutedness' and silence do not imply static subjugation to the status quo. Instead, the process "by which women are rendered 'mute' or manage to construct dissenting genres and resisting discourses" (1991: 190) should be a feature of research. In other words, Gal called for a more positive valuation of silence than has been traditionally practised. The thread that runs through all of Gal's contributions is the idea of *competing ideologies at the site of discursive interactions.* The structure of the political economy provides the context that makes sense of both the linguistic events and the participants' behaviour. Whether in silence or in talk, people engage in a kind of continual struggle for their right to define 'reality'.

My purpose is to study particular instances of language use with the view to understand the interconnections between linguistic resources, social identities, cultural prejudices, and political-ideological viewpoints. The individuals focused on here are United States Supreme Court judges, and the data to be examined are the judicial opinions which are attributed to these judges. I seek an understanding of how these particular judges function in their specific judicial contexts, both in their capacities as individuals with personal beliefs and ideologies, and as legal officers acting within the constraints of a powerful institution, as well as as members of American society and culture at particular periods in time and history.

2.3 *Language and gender discrimination*

Apart from being a book about judicial rhetoric, this is also a book about gender discrimination and women's rights, and the attitudes of the American

Supreme Court towards these issues. A feminist theory of law is thus a crucial perspective that must be included in the present enterprise.

Current debates in feminist legal theory may be broadly classified along the lines of four key issues: equality, difference, dominance, and women's voices. The concept of equality is increasingly questioned as "a problematic foundation for legal reform" (Bartlett and Kennedy 1991:5). Known also as the assimilationist view, the questions posed in equality debates are: "Do women want simply to be treated like men?" or, "What does it mean to pursue equality in a society stratified by income, education, race, physical and mental ability, and age – as well as gender?" (Bartlett and Kennedy 1991:5). Through the experiences of the numerous court battles in recent years involving pregnancy-related issues and women's living conditions after divorce, legal scholars are no longer sure that the demand for equal treatment can really gain for women the justice that they seek, given that inherent social stratifications have placed the sexes on an unequal footing from the start. However, to ask for special treatment is to risk the paternalist traditional protection for women, and as a result, scholars have found the issue not to be easily resolvable one way or the other.

The assimilationist view is opposed by the difference view, which argues that the sexes are not "similarly situated" and hence cannot be treated as equals. Instead, the call in the difference camp is for recognizing and celebrating gender differences. However, as Martha Minow (1987:13–14) has rightly pointed out,

> [l]egal treatment of difference tends to take for granted an assumed point of comparison: women are compared to the unstated norm of men . . [and it] tends to treat as unproblematic the point of view from which difference is seen, assigned, or ignored, rather than acknowledging that the problem of difference can be described and understood from multiple points of view.

The problem is that whether similarities or differences are foregrounded in these debates, the point of reference remains implicitly the male point of view, a viewpoint that has proven more difficult to dissociate from than has been generally recognized. Worden (1985:1144, 1146) defined the problem as follows:

> The injustice is that society has historically chosen to recognize only the "male voice." This has resulted in the subjugation, silencing, and misunderstanding of the "female voice" in both men and women. This ideological prejudice is acutely evident in law and legal education. As noted by Sheila McIntyre, "[g]oing to

> law school is learning to speak male as a second language, and learning it fluently". . Unless you think and speak "their" language, you have inferior capabilities. If you try to speak your own language, you won't be understood (unless "translated") and will feel stupid and embarrassed for having spoken up. Moreover, if you are "lucky" enough to be translated, it is more likely than not that the rich texture of your comment will be distorted or lost in the translation.

Carrie Menkel-Meadow (1987:29) echoed the same sentiment that women's exclusion from participation in the law imposes upon women as a class the need to access "both its own world and the world of the oppressor". In other words, women are forced to become "multilingual, speaking white, male, objective tongues, while at the same time speaking in black, brown, yellow, red, female, and subjective ones". However, Menkel-Meadow (1987:43, 50, 52) emphasizes the potential *positive* results that can be derived from such an exclusion:

> We, the excluded, should learn from our exclusion that our insights and ways of doing things are valuable and can be transformative . . our common exclusions may enable us to see that there is a vision of equality that does not require sameness, that there is glory in diversity and difference, and that there are ways for the law to include, accommodate, and rejoice in the social and cultural differences that both enrich our society as well as threaten to divide it. . Such is the lesson of the knowledge of exclusion – that each time we let in a new excluded group, that each time we listen to a new way of knowing, we learn more about the limits of our current ways of seeing. Rather than being threatened by new entrants into the legal profession and the law, we should be grateful for the opportunity to learn that perhaps there are new and other ways to do things.

Another major strand in feminist scholarship is Catharine MacKinnon's work on dominance. In MacKinnon's view, debates on sexual differences and equality are misplaced and attention should instead be directed at identifying arenas of male dominance and female subordination. MacKinnon (1984:90, italics added) differentiates her approach from the difference view as follows:

> If you follow my shift in perspective from gender as difference to gender as dominance, gender changes from a distinction that is presumptively valid to a detriment that is presumptively suspect. *The difference approach tries to map reality; the dominance approach tries to challenge and change it. In the dominance approach, sex discrimination stops being a question of morality and starts being a question of politics.*

MacKinnon's dominance view represents a rejection of the difference-equality debates as based on an inherent contradiction. Her formulation of the problem of gender in the law as an issue of dominance and oppression has taken feminist legal scholarship out of the plane of the merely biological and socio-cultural into the realm of the political.

What is shared in these debates in feminist jurisprudence is this: in their own ways, each of them seeks to question and challenge the status quo. From the demand for equal treatment to the challenge posed to male dominance, these strands of feminist critique work at the demolition of the patriarchal myth that "the domination of women is a natural right, a mere reflection of the biological family" (Scales 1986: 1379). While feminist legal scholarship has contributed significantly to unveiling the androcentrism of law, society and culture, however, the internal disagreements and the less-than-assured guarantee of justice for women have necessitated continued self-examination and critique of both feminist theories and practice.

I am in agreement with Patricia Cain (1990) that impressive as the achievements had been, current feminist legal theory excludes non-mainstream women who do not speak the dominant discourse. In other words, feminist jurisprudence speaks only for mainstream white women, and does not address the problems faced by women of colour. Although the first tenet of feminist jurisprudence was, and still is, to draw from the lives of women and to listen more attentively to different female voices, the theoretical debates and intra-disciplinary splits within feminist jurisprudence have perhaps caused an unintended distancing from the primary issue – the importance of the female subjects of all races and classes, their shared experiences as well as the differences in their social and political conditions.

In addition, feminist legal scholarship also does not show sufficient concern for the nature of legal discourse, the legal institution and the world in which these are embedded. It is important to study the discourse of the dominant culture simply because women's experiences are still articulated within the terms of the dominant discourse. As Minow (1987: 15) has said,

> justice is made by people who live in a world already made. Existing institutions and language already carve the world and already express and recreate attitudes about what counts as a difference, and who or what is the relevant point of comparison.

Unfortunately, still largely applicable to our world today are Susan B. Anthony's words that "forms of law [are] all made by men, interpreted by men, administered by men, in favor of men, and against women" (Stanton et al. 1881:688). I believe that we need to refocus our concerns on the site of legal struggles, i.e., in women's experiences and institutional discourse. The emphasis on women's experiences, however, is currently at the centre of another relatively new and burgeoning trend in feminist legal scholarship, whose focus is on women's narratives.[3]

Kathryn Abrams (1994:44) discusses the motivations that lie behind the growth of feminist narrative scholarship:

> The valuation of experiential knowledge, the conviction that the exclusion of women's perspectives has distorted the development of legal rules, and a growing frustration with the abstraction and distance conventionally required of legal decisionmakers have produced a wave of women's storytelling. Authors use their own experiential stories, or those of others, to illuminate what unites and divides us across lines of gender, race, class, or sexual orientation. They offer these stories not only to illuminate the insights that have been excluded, but to help legal decisionmakers develop less partial, more broadly responsive legal solutions.

Though feminist narrative scholarship has met with different kinds of resistance (Abrams 1994:47ff.), especially from mainstream legal scholars who have expressed doubts about the value of personal narratives in contributing to legal reforms, its concern over reforming the traditionally male perspectives adopted by the law through forcing the courts and legislatures to confront the real-life experiences of woman as victim, woman as other, and women's relationships as peripheral, is a step taken in the right direction. In this type of scholarship, life and law meet in the ethnographic context of narratives. Such an approach more closely approximates to the stated aim of feminist jurisprudence to listen attentively to women's voices, and to re-centre women's voices in legal narratives.

One of my goals is to demonstrate the multifaceted interpenetrations of different strands of discursive practices (whether social, political, personal, institutional, or ideological). It is not sufficient to ground statements in more global theories of social and political economy. Instead, this global perspective of the wider contexts of discourse production and interpretation must be balanced by a situated investigation of the local linguistic practices of the culture or group to be studied. Therefore, I adopt an *eclectic* approach in this book: on the one hand, contextualizing my analysis globally in wider theories of social and political economy, and on the other hand, locating my analysis at the most local level of linguistic usage – the language of judges as manifested in the text, cotext, and context of the particular society and culture.

3. The road to be taken

This book addresses issues that lie at the intersection of discourse, gender, ideology, power and law, and the interconnections between them. In a nutshell, discourse is viewed as the actual use of language in the context of community and culture. In actual acts of daily discourses, members of a community congregate to engage in an on-going and ever-evolving process of linguistic and social negotiation. Hence, by focusing on the discourse of the community (in this case, the discourse of the community of American Supreme Court judges), the history and character of the community as enacted through discourse is to be elucidated. The perspective adopted here is thus both socially-constituted and discourse-centred, i.e., one that insists on the notion that the life and history of a community are crucially inscribed and expressed in their discourse.

My data sample of four judicial opinions from four United States Supreme Court cases share an important feature: each is a case involving gender issues. One of the aims of this project is to understand and chart the developmental history of the changing legal status of American women. For this reason, U.S. Supreme Court cases involving women who challenged laws that excluded women's participation are chosen. This book is therefore also a *feminist* enterprise: it promotes critical awareness regarding the issue of gender discrimination in American society and addresses the matter of judicial responses and attitudes to such charges of discrimination. I suggest a way in which we can come to grasp the nature of the discrimination and the rhetoric of law that has played such an important role in this kind of discourse. In this spirit, the language of the judicial opinions is examined from various standpoints; the main argument I propose centres around the very important role that language plays in defining and inscribing women's legal existence and rights. In this way, the centrality of language in the law and in gender discrimination is to be brought out here.

I build upon the research that has been established by scholars in gender studies by emphasizing the social and political contexts in my analysis. The judicial texts will be situated against the backdrop of other judicial texts, conventions of legal discourse, and institutional rules as well as the surrounding socio-political and ideological milieu that contribute to their production and interpretation. The judge is viewed in his/her role as a judge situated in the context of the legal institution, as an individual living in the society and as a product of his/her culture. Both the local and the global contexts must be a part of the description in order that a holistic account of the production and interpretation of texts in the political economy can be achieved. My primary goal then is to show how language usage, gender dynamics, ideology and power structures converge and are negotiated and contested in these judicial texts.

The role of ideology in this complex interplay of issues is central. As an institutional discourse of power, judicial rhetoric is simultaneously driven by several kinds of ideologies. At the local level of *personal/individual ideology*, the judge is a person with specific personal commitments to and investments in the world he/she inhabits. At the same time, the judge is an officer of the law, and in his/her capacity as a judge, he/she is to some extent dictated by the agendas of the legal institution. This is the level of *institutional ideology*. The judge is, finally, also a member situated in his/her society at particular time periods in American social and legal history just as the legal institution is an important social institution in the American socio-cultural and political milieu; hence the need to consider the *socio-cultural and political ideology*. Sited among these different ideological levels are potential areas of conflict and consensus, thus giving rise to the idea of freedom and constraints.

In the judicial context, there is also the question of power – the power that judges are entrusted with to interpret the laws of the land; and the power of judges to effect decisions in some specific directions. In short, judicial power is the power of knowledge construction – the power to define and inscribe the rights of American citizens.

And finally, there is the question of law itself. The issues to be dealt with in this book are legal issues in the following sense: the data are cases (of gender discrimination); the language dealt with is a special form of legal discourse (judicial opinions); the issues discussed involve the power of judges and institutions in determining the rights of American women. Law is itself a form of rhetoric, a mode of reasoning and a crucial arm of the social institution. This book hopes to bring out the intricate connections between the micro categories (discourse) and the macro constructs (gender, ideology, power and law). To do this, I propose to examine judicial discourse from four different perspectives, i.e., I am advocating in this book the adoption of a *multi-disciplinary* viewpoint.

The ideas that directly influence my analysis are: Elinor Ochs' (1992) model which effects the connections between language and gender; Robert Benson's (1988) proposal for interpreting law as a semiotic web of resources; Michel Foucault's ideas of discourse, power and knowledge construction; and an ethnographic approach to language, law and culture (see Chapter Two). Running through these four perspectives is a common thread: whether viewed from a linguistic, semiotic, ethnographic, or discursive-ideological perspective, at the centre of all these lies the *constitutive role of language*. By harmonizing these four perspectives in the present context, I hope to accomplish three goals: (1) to argue for the need for multidisciplinarity; (2) to show the complex relationships that permeate the issues raised here; (3) to offer as a case in point the richness of such a characterization that effect a more accurate representation of judicial realities.

Chapters Three and Four aim to fulfill two major goals. One, through an analysis of the language of the judicial opinions, I demonstrate how law with respect to gender discrimination can be viewed from a multidisciplinary viewpoint. Two, through a discussion of the issues that are raised by these four cases, I provide a historical understanding of the interplay between gender, law, and ideology.

The cases selected for this project are thus cases involving aspects of sex discrimination against women. These four cases are also selected for the period they were situated. The first pair of cases (*Bradwell v. Illinois, 1872* and *Muller v. Oregon, 1908*) represents the High Court's treatment of gender issues in the early years of American legal history. The second pair of cases (*Reed v. Reed, 1971* and *Roe v. Wade, 1973*) provides an opportunity to witness the more contemporary judicial rhetoric regarding gender discrimination. Together, they give us a glimpse of how America's highest court treat gender issues through those years. The basic argument is that though the judicial rhetoric has indeed changed and developed phenomenally, there is still a lot more that the Court can do to bring about a more liberating atmosphere for women through the power of judicial discursive innovation.

The language of judicial opinions is examined in terms of both a *synchronic* view of situated language use and a *diachronic* view of the discursive shifts through time and socio-cultural changes. My project is thus an attempt at a detailed trace of both the localized use of language and the global contextualization of interactions. In what has been appropriately labelled as a "vocabulary of motive" (Mills 1940), my work seeks to track not just the vocabulary, but also the grammar, the semantics and the rhetorical structuring of motives that go into the making of a judicial text, and by implication of text or discourse as a micro-inscription of the story of a culture and of communal life. In essence, my ultimate goal is to characterize (laden with my own set of ideological commitments, I will admit) the linguistic, legal, and socio-cultural ideologies in nineteenth and twentieth century America.

The concluding chapter contains four sections. The first section summarizes the ideas that permeate the book. This book as a whole deals with the rhetorical construction of women's rights. It also deals with the power of judges to effect such linguistic constructions. I argue that though social, cultural and ideological changes ride in tandem with the linguistic changes, it is the changes effected in the discourse of judges that provide an important source of actual societal changes in the making. In other words, the power of discourse to define, create and effect social changes cannot be overemphasized or underestimated.

The second section addresses the specific issue of crossing disciplinary lines. As the subject of this book involves multiple disciplines (law, gender, ideology, language), I see the need for a multidisciplinary framework that will give a comprehensive characterization of the relationships between these issues. However, crossing disciplinary borders is not an endeavour that everyone can/will embrace wholeheartedly. In this section then, I reiterate the need and, indeed, the importance of incorporating multidisciplinary viewpoints in the present context, and for that matter, in contexts beyond the covers of any one book. We, as individuals and as scholars, have for a long time chosen, unwisely, to limit ourselves by staying within the boundaries of our own worlds or disciplines. It is time to realize that such self-imposed exclusion can only be a short-sighted and solipsistic vision of our research enterprise and an unnecessary exile. The knowledge explosion has shown us how disciplinary concerns are, in fact, closer to each other than we think, and we should exploit the new access to knowledge in terms of information transfer and current technologies to open our minds to others who harbour similar concerns. I recall once again, Wittgenstein's ominous pronouncement that "[t]he limits of my language mean the limits of my world". If we only expand that language by 'languaging' between and across the disciplines, the physical and psychological boundaries of our world need not pose obstacles to our search for multidisciplinary understanding and knowledge.

In the third section, I address the issue of ethnographic standing. Approaching law and gender discrimination in the American context from the viewpoint of a 'non-native', it is necessary to provide a defence of the validity and value of such a viewpoint. In this section, I also question the distinction between 'native' and 'non-native', my view being that this distinction is no longer an interesting one, and in fact, in the reality of today's world, a dichotomy that has become highly problematic. I conclude this section by discussing the kinds of contribution this work and its particular linguistic viewpoint on law, gender and ideology can make to disciplines external to linguistics.

In the final section, I identify the future challenges for feminist jurisprudence in the years ahead. The questions raised here include: (1) given what we know about how the Court operates with respect to women's issues, what should feminist jurisprudence aim to do? (2) what are the issues that still need to be addressed and what are the agendas that feminists in general still need to push for? In this final section, I offer my thoughts on issues of equality, rights and justice for the two sexes.

Chapter 2

Towards multidisciplinarity

Gendered discourse, judicial ideologies and the power of law

1. Discourse, gender, ideology, power and law

> [There are] three themes that I take to be fundamental to sociolinguistics: first, that there is a mode of organization of language that is a part of the organization of communicative conduct in a community, whose understanding requires a corresponding, new mode of description of language; second, that recognition of this mode of organization leads one to recognize that the study of language is a multidisciplinary field, a field to which ordinary linguistics is indispensable, but to which other disciplines, such as sociology, social anthropology, education, folklore, and poetics, are indispensable as well; third, that study of this mode of organization leads one to reconsider the bases of linguistics itself. One might say that the three themes have to do with the scope, the dependencies, and, ultimately, the foundations of linguistics.
>
> –Dell Hymes (1974a: vii-viii)

I am committed to a multidisciplinary approach because of: (1) the nature of my goal, which is to achieve as full a characterization as is possible of the nature of the discourse of judges and, (2) the complex nature of law, which may be viewed in at least four ways, which I will explain below.

To provide a comprehensive interpretation of socio-political ideology as manifested in the text, we would have to take into account the different aspects of text-making. To understand the nature of life as it is lived in a particular community, we must be sensitive not just to the everyday activities as they unfold before our eyes; we must also focus on the community's history, religious and social practices and beliefs, institutional and individual personalities and prejudices, public opinion, and even the nature of its institutions. Only when we, as observers of a culture, have developed some kind of understanding of the structure and the norms of a society, from the habits of its individuals to the complexities of its institutions, can we be said to have tapped into the "temper" of the culture (Jane Belo's term, 1970, cited by Geertz

1973: 417). However, while such an attempt at a full characterization is sought here, I agree with James Clifford's qualification that "the whole picture" is in practice not achievable.[1] As a linguist examining legal/judicial discourse through the window of select opinions issued by the judges of the U.S. Supreme Court, my field of vision is also limited; nevertheless it offers possibilities for understanding the judicial culture.

The second motivation for multidisciplinarity stems from the complex nature of law itself. In most democratic societies, and in both literate and non-literate cultures, the law and legal institutions may be conceived of in at least four ways. First, law as the ethnographic telling and retelling of the story of a culture has been described in the following way:

> Law, like every other cultural institution, is a place where we tell one another stories about our relationships with ourselves, one another, and authority. . When we tell one another stories, we use languages and themes that different pieces of the culture make available to us, and that limit the stories we can tell. Since our stories influence how we imagine, as well as how we describe, our relationships, our stories also limit who we can be (Dalton 1988: 285).

In other words, in the language of law lies the constitution and reconstitution of the life and history of a community. Every existing law in a particular society is not an isolated instantiation of socio-cultural and political-ideological practice. Instead, each law, enshrined in each statute, is the result of a lengthy process of discursive negotiation by the people (or at least by the ones who are privileged enough to be parties in such negotiations) belonging to the culture. As such, each statute is a manifestation of the values, beliefs and ideology of the society, or at least of some dominant section of the society. By carefully examining the language of the law, then, I believe an understanding of the nature of the culture in question can be achieved. Law is, in this sense, an inscription of the story of the culture.

Second, law as rhetoric may also be seen as a literary activity. Law as rhetoric means to "expose the way law shapes all stories into particular patterns of telling, favors certain stories and disfavors others, or even makes it impossible to tell certain kinds of stories" (Dalton 1988: 285). Far from being the distant and mysterious entity that the general public views it to be, the law is just another kind of social activity (though an important kind) and an arena for negotiating the terms by which individuals belonging to a community are expected to live. The legal text, like a literary text, is thus open to scrutiny. Also, like any literary text, the law is a text that is composed (as opposed to 'already made') by real people, and is always subject to change through a process of re-formulation and reinterpretation. In short, law is an active, ever-evolving and dynamic process; it is not immutable but is authoritative only insofar as the ones responsible for its being allows it to be so.

A third possibility of viewing the law and the language of the law is to see them as indices of both legal and socio-cultural ideology. If law is a crucial part of life and history, then the language of the law is an index of what that life and history are about. Law is thus viewed as ethnography at two levels. First, the law as expressed in judicial opinions is ethnographic in its characterization of the legal and social relations of the community from the judicial viewpoint. Second, the perspective on law adopted here is also ethnographic in the sense that my own description of the judicial view of communal life is situated in the social, legal and cultural contexts of judicial text production. In the language of the law is thus inscribed the story of communal life (judicial, social, and political) from specific (internal and external) viewpoints.

There is, in addition, a fourth way to looking at legal activities – law as a semiotic web of meanings (Benson 1988).[2] The advantage of the idea of a semiotic web lies in it being "a metaphor which sees the individual surrounded by a cultural web of signs" (Benson 1988:38). The lawmaker is thus an individual situated in this complex interconnected network of signs, acting simultaneously as a sign reader, a sign maker, and a sign interpreter. Conceptualizing law as a sign system (Kevelson 1988) thus has the added richness of foregrounding law as a paradigmatic system of potential choices one can draw from in the legal writing and reading process. Also, law as a sign network emphasizes at the same time that each instance of manifestation in the actualized syntagm (say, a legal text) is the result of the specific linguistic (i.e. lexical, grammatical, semantic, discursive) choices made through a multitude of possibilities that have now been assembled in the text.

2. The different uses of 'discourse'

The term 'discourse' and the method of linguistic inquiry called 'discourse analysis' have been used in various ways by different linguists. In the days when the concerns of grammarians terminate at the sentence or the clause level, the study of 'bigger' or 'higher' units of language (longer stretches of speech and writing, for instance) is delegated to other analysts. The growing need to account for linguistic interactions over and above the level of the clause (that is, the need to recognize the existence and realities of paragraphs, dialogues, and anything that stretches for more than one clause length), however, has forced more and more linguists to look constantly for new ways of analysis.

In one tradition of British linguistics, the Birmingham school, 'discourse' is associated only with *oral* linguistic exchanges, and is used in this context to designate a level of analysis that is higher in rank than the sentence. 'Discourse analysis' is hence the method of analysis which characterizes entire classroom exchanges into moves and acts (Sinclair and Coulthard 1975; Coulthard and Montgomery 1982).

The idea of 'discourse' as a higher unit than the clause is also central in Hallidayan linguistics. Taking its cues from the Firthian tradition (1957, which goes all the way back to Bronislaw Malinowski), Michael Halliday privileges meaning and what is called, the 'context of situation'. Halliday (1978, 1985/1994, Halliday and Martin (eds) 1981; also see Benson, Cummings and Greaves (eds) 1988) divides language into a three-tiered system of phonology, lexicogrammar and discourse. The level of discourse is not just a 'bigger' unit (a question of level size), but is also a 'higher' and separate level of analysis (the concept of rank). For Halliday, 'discourse' is both spoken and written. Attention is paid not just to classroom talk, but extends also to stretches of discourse as widely differing as literary genres and therapeutic discourse. In this framework, 'discourse analysis' is concerned with interpreting the social meaning of language in context. J.R. Martin (1989), among others, has also focused on the political meanings inherent in discourse. Hallidayan scholars are, therefore, engaged in detailing the paradigmatic potentials of the linguistic system and the social and political functions of syntagmatic realizations within the network of a semantic-grammar of discursive choices. It should be noted that the East Anglian school of critical linguistics (Fowler et al. 1979, Hodge and Kress 1979, 1988; and Kress 1989), which focuses on ideological readings of discourse, has largely been based on the assumptions of Hallidayan linguistics.

Yet another use of 'discourse' is Deborah Tannen's "unified approach" (1982c). Tannen defines 'discourse' as "language in context across all forms and modes" (1982c: x). Hence, 'discourse' is both spoken and written. Spoken or oral discourse is traditionally also known by the label "talk," and written discourse is also called "text" (Cicourel 1975, for example). However,

Tannen's unified approach to discourse means that the boundary between talk and text is blurred, and is, in fact, not easily separable. Maintaining that "[f]eatures that have been associated exclusively with spoken or written language are often found in discourse of the other mode" (1982c: x), Tannen rejects the demarcation of talk as oral and text as written as untenable (Tannen 1982a, b, c).

Joel Sherzer's use of 'discourse', shared also by Greg Urban (1991), is based on Hymes' ethnography of speaking in that 'discourse' is said to be a constitutive part of social interaction. Instead of it being just another level of analysis, 'discourse' is, most importantly, the means which shapes communal life and defines experience and history, and is the medium in which cultural logic is expressed. This particular emphasis on the constitutive nature of discourse, which is lacking in earlier conceptions, is extremely important because it locates discourse or language in the midst of culture and society, thus echoing the Sapir-Whorf view of the interpenetration of language and worldview. In addition, Sherzer's very important distinction between 'grammar' and 'discourse' must be emphasized:

> discourse has a structure and a patterning of its own, related to but separate from grammar, . . it draws on and utilizes the resources provided by grammar in ways that shed most interesting light on grammar itself. More generally, there is increasing recognition that discourse is not only the place of the actualization of grammar, but the place of the creation of grammar (1990: 5).

Michel Foucault's concept of 'discourse' may be distinguished from all the above in that Foucauldian 'discourse' is spoken of in relation to the much more abstract concept of "discursive formations" (Foucault 1972, 1972–1977, 1978). 'Discourse' is thus bound up in power relations and knowledge structures, a view that has been more recently expressed within linguistics by, for example, Norman Fairclough (1992).

My perspective accepts the social and ideological nature of discourse as espoused by Hallidayan and critical linguists. I also recognize the problematics of the oral-written distinction that Tannen's unified approach suggests. In addition, I agree with Sherzer's and Urban's idea of 'discourse' as constitutive of social encounters. Finally, my perspective also embraces Foucault's discursive formations within the network of knowledge and power.

3. Multiple frameworks

3.1 Indexing gender and ideology

Elinor Ochs (1992) develops a model that makes linkages between discourse and gender, via an intermediate plane of social stances, acts and activities. The three levels – discourse, gender and social activities – are linked by two kinds of indexical relations, called direct indexical relations and indirect indexical relations. According to Ochs (1992: 343),

> This model puts gender in its place, indicating that it enters into complex constitutive relations with other categories of social meaning. Indeed the model indicates that gender is not the only category of social meaning that may be impacted by a different social domain.

Useful as Ochs' model is for my attempt to link judicial discourse to the culture, it is however not broad enough to encompass my goal. Silverstein's (1985) discussion of ideology is instructive in filling this gap.

Michael Silverstein (1985) argues that to characterize properly the relationship between language, gender, and culture, we must take into consideration three separate but interlocking perspectives, which he labels the structural, the pragmatic, and the ideological (p.221). It is possible that what Silverstein calls the "structural realm", defined as linguistic forms, is what Ochs calls "linguistic resources" or what Sherzer calls "grammar". Though it is tempting to associate Silverstein's "pragmatic realm" with Ochs' intermediate level of stances, acts and activities, I would hesitate to make such a hasty conflation. In fact, as Silverstein defines the pragmatic realm as "usage as discourse in actual situations of communication", I am reminded once again of the Sherzerian sense of 'discourse' as concrete linguistic usage.

What I find particularly useful in Silverstein's work is the ideological realm that is lacking (at least explicitly) in both Ochs and Sherzer. A study in ideology, the "conscious purposivity in language use" (Silverstein 1985: 222–223), will shed light on the "why?" in judicial text production. Incorporating Silverstein's ideological realm and Ochs' idea of indexical relations into my present concerns, I arrive at my own diagrammatic representation of how gender, power and ideological relations are mapped (Fig. 1).

My six-tiered model shows how language indexes social activities and roles, gender relations, law, society and ideology, and how these categories are in their turn reflected in the deployment of linguistic resources. Locating

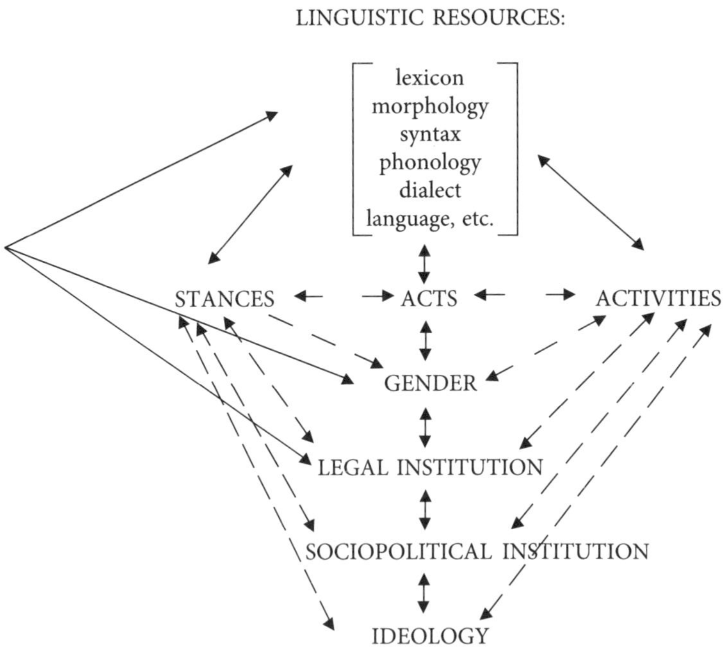

Figure 1. Linguistic indexing of gender, power, and ideology

ideology at the lowest tier is not just an intentional and iconic attempt to image the gulf (in terms of the complexities of tiers: linguistic, social, biological and sexual, legal, social and political) that separates ideology from linguistic resources, but also to convey the sense that ideology is totalizing, in the sense that it is everywhere and that it encompasses and pervades all the levels above it. The restriction imposed by a two-dimensional representation is such that it is difficult to place ideology anywhere in the diagram that will show that it penetrates every realm of our lives. A better way to picture ideology is on a three-dimensional plane with ideology hovering above all the five tiers, with radiating arrows connecting all these tiers to it.

3. 2 The semiotic view of law

According to Robert Benson, "[a] pragmatic account of legal interpretation will have to start . . with the modernist notion that language and legal meaning are cultural artifacts produced in time and space through specific social institutions" (1988: 38).[3] As such, the main advantage of the idea of a semiotic web is that it places the individual at the centre of the influences on life in the community. Each potential influence or sign carries with it its own web of associations, significations and repercussions as each of them refers, implicates, and influences other signs in the web. In this web of cultural meanings, both the individual (the meaning maker) and the language (as (socio)-linguistic resource and meaning potential) are intricately linked and they mutually impinge on each other in a network of a potentially limitless Peircean semiosis (Peirce 1931–1935).

The reader has to interact with the text(s) that he/she is reading or interpreting. In the case of the judicial reader, the choice of texts ranges from the legal (from the oral arguments), judicial (other judges' discourse), the legislative (lawmakers' input), or the constitutional (the U.S. Constitution itself), etc. Depending on the reader, and the type of texts chosen by him/her, different kinds of meanings may come into play. For example, some readers treat constitutional texts as having a fixed and plain meaning. In other words, the meanings of constitutional texts are often taken to be easily 'read off' from just looking at what is written. There are, of course, other kinds of readers who would dispute the existence of a plain textual meaning, and who would treat constitutional texts as yet another kind of texts whose meanings are open to interpretation and change.[4]

The reader has also to consider what Benson calls "source of text". By this is meant the individuals and circumstances which contribute to the production of texts, and which provide the conditions for their production. Applying this to the judicial opinions, these conditions include factors like the individual intentions and the styles of the judges, the socio-cultural climate of text production, and so on.

Yet another key influence on the reader is the presence of other readers. More specifically, this factor raises the issue of "public meanings" (Benson 1988: 49) and the need to communicate within a community of readers, writers, and speakers. In the judicial context, this factor translates into the pressure exerted on the judicial reader by other judges and the public audience. Under the sway of public opinion, or influenced by fellow colleagues on the bench, the judicial author/reader may act in some ways rather than another.

The reader also experiences various pressures within his/her own core. Such internal considerations include the reader's own history and personal values. In the case of judicial readers, Benson points out that personal ideology and values are "at work in the judges' heads" (p.51). Hence, the political affiliation of the judge is an important factor that needs to be considered in acts of interpretation, reading and writing.

Benson's ideas provide a useful way to think about the distinct yet interlocking factors that operate in the interpretive and writing process. Grouping the different factors that Benson mentions into three main categories, the individual, the socio-cultural, and the institutional, facilitates both ease of discussion and also provides a sharper picture of how the different factors relate to one another on distinct levels, arising from the person of the judge, the society itself and the legal institution. From these ideas, I arrive at the following mapping of how individual, socio-cultural and institutional factors are at play, simultaneously exerting influences on the reader-judge, who is situated at the centre of the semiotic web.

Figure 2 shows three main categories: the individual, the socio-cultural

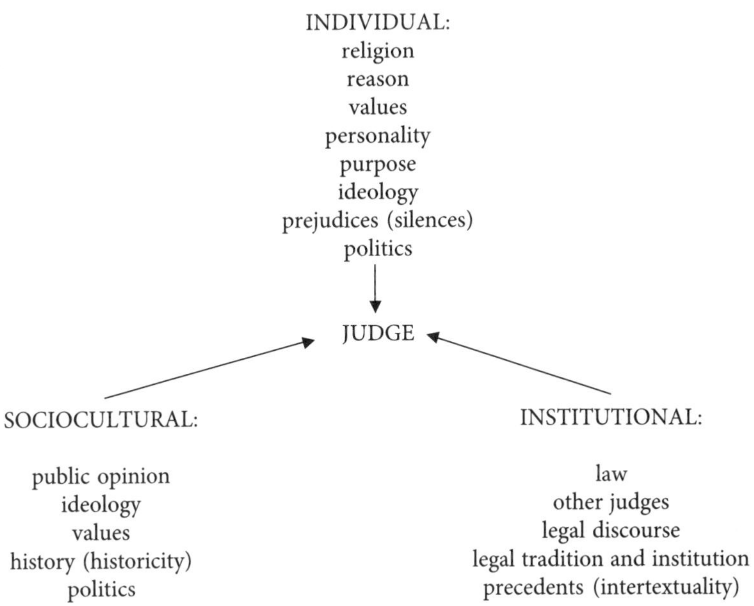

Figure 2. A semiotic web of resources: choices and constraints in the production and interpretation of the judicial opinion

and the institutional. Within the individual level are factors such as the judge's personality, beliefs, and political affiliations that I think will directly influence the judge in choosing one path rather than another in the reading and writing of texts. Two other external levels, social and political forces, also exert pressure on the judicial actor. This includes public opinions and the history of the culture. This consideration recognizes that judges operate within a certain contextual frame that arises from the society and culture in which they are members, though the choice is still open to judges to either agree with public and social sentiments or to oppose them. The third level of potential influence comes from the legal institution itself. The constraints of legal and judicial discourse, and the ground rules determining all aspects of judicial behaviour and performance, for example, both bear on the judge as he/she reads, interprets, and eventually writes his/her opinion. Together, these three levels act simultaneously and sometimes, insidiously, to influence judicial decisions, and thus, an understanding of the workings of the semiotic web of resources will prove valuable in my characterization of the ideological motives that propel judicial text production. Judicial performance is, however, not as highly constrained an activity as this brief explanation of the workings of the web may have suggested. There is, in fact, both freedom and constraint, in any act of judicial performance.

The emic-etic distinction has been applied to law by legal critics in terms of the difference between the legal practitioner's 'objective' view of law as unchanging legal principles and dictates that are "fixed by the touchstone of authorial intent" (Benson 1988: 34) and the (realist) critic's view of law that insists on the fluidity and dynamic nature of textual meanings. Due to their very indeterminate nature, legal meanings manifested in legal discourse are argued to be subject to individual interpretation, which is couched in particular spatial and temporal contexts. In Benson's words (1988: 34):

> the legal materials themselves are indeterminate. It is the judges, working like artists producing a collage, who assemble the materials into a work that they create in their own minds and then display for the public in the form of a written opinion.

The 'problem' with the realist view is simple: judges are not convinced!

Ronald Dworkin's (1982) famous metaphor, which illustrates the predetermined nature of legal textual meanings, involves a "chain gang enterprise". The chain gang enterprise consists of a number of writers, assembled to write a novel collaboratively, the understanding being that each writer writes one chapter based on the earlier chapters that have already been written by the other members. Dworkin's point is that in such a chain enterprise, only the first author is free to write as he/she pleases; the subsequent writers are constrained by what has already been established by the ones who came before him/her. When applied to the creation of the judicial opinion, what this means is that judges are constrained to write in a prescribed way long established by the legal institution. What is claimed here is that legal interpretation, and hence writing, being highly constrained, is thus based objectively in what the law says, and not in how judges intend the law to be. There is then no room, in this view, for judicial variation and innovation.

I find this objectivist view and the trust put in the objectivity of the law to be naïve. As Stanley Fish says, it is indeed "tempting to think that the more information one has (the more history) the more directed will be one's interpretation", but as Fish further cautions, "information only comes in an interpreted form (it does not announce itself)" (1989:90). Therefore, the first writer in the chain is just as constrained (by how to start a novel) as it is equally true that the other subsequent members are just as free to continue the tale in the ways that they please, though admittedly this latter freedom can only be wielded within certain bounds. Fish concludes, and I think his is the correct conclusion, that Dworkin is mistaken that writers, first or last, can be "neither free nor constrained". Instead they are all "free *and* constrained" at the same instant (Fish 1989:89).

The judicial opinion, like the novel, has to be written in a certain way, due to generic and institutional rules. But even under these circumstances, the judge is, nevertheless, free to innovate through various linguistic means, as I will show in my analysis. In short, the judicial author, not unlike the chain writers, enjoys the same freedom to create and is bound by similar constraints to adhere by institutional norms, these rules being applicable to them all by virtue of their professed affiliation to the same institution. In fact, even in the individual exercise of freedom that may result in the violation of rules, this violation still has to take note of the rule that it is violating (Fish 1989:89).

3.3 An ethnographic perspective on legal discourse

Sherzer (1989:269) allocates to language a central role in shaping the world-view of any culture:

> A central aspect of culture is the logic, the world view, and the symbols by means

> of which a group of people perceive and conceive of the world. Language is central to this view of culture. Language is the verbal means by which individuals conceive of, express, and transmit culture.

Sherzer's use of "logic" draws our attention to all the cultural tidbits that contribute to the internal coherences that constitute the culture in question. This foregrounds an important sense of relativity between cultures: what makes sense to one does not always, and in fact will most likely not, make sense in another cultural context. In this way, every culture is unique, and the linguistic system that is peculiar to each culture plays a decisive role in making the difference real.

By "language" Sherzer means "discourse", which lies at "the nexus, the actual and concrete expression of the language-culture-society relationship" (Sherzer 1987: 296). Sherzer's idea of 'discourse' is a concept that refers concretely to the sung lyrics in the curing chants of the Kuna Indians (1983) and even though Sherzer has not included them in his own work, 'discourse' also encompasses the written words of a printed text.

It is not as trite as it might seem to observe that language (in Sherzer's sense) plays a far greater and deeper part than mere words can capture. Language is at once individual and social, idiosyncratic and shared, a vehicle for communication and an instrument for expressing and influencing thought. In addition, language is the means and the medium for transmitting ideas and experiences. Given the immense importance of language to individuals and cultures, a method of analysis like Sherzer's that privileges actual forms of usage hits right at the site of the activities that define the society and culture.

In proposing to add an ethnographic angle to this study of judicial performance, I believe there is a need at this juncture to provide an argument for the ethnographic status of the present work. I follow various well-established practices in identifying what I believe is central to the ethnographic enterprise. In particular, Clifford Geertz's advice, in his essay, "From the Native's Point of View" (1983), is most instructive:

> The trick is not to get yourself into some inner correspondence of spirit with your informants. Preferring, like the rest of us, to call their souls their own, they are not going to be altogether keen about such effort anyhow. The trick is to figure out what the devil they think they are up to (Geertz 1983: 58).

In claiming that I am doing ethnography in my study of judicial performance, I am certainly *not* saying that I have any direct access to the judges in question, much less that I am "into some inner correspondence of spirit" with them! What I do have access to is the written text of the judicial opinions. These are central to judicial performance, and are also important sources of judicial thinking on all sorts of issues. Hence, even though I have no direct access to my judicial subjects, I do have access to ways of trying to understand "what the devil they think they are up to".

Alessandro Duranti wrote of ethnography that it is "a style in which the researcher establishes a dialogue between different viewpoints and voices, including those of the people studied, of the ethnographer, and of his disciplinary and theoretical preferences" (1997: 87). Establishing different viewpoints and letting different voices speak are exactly what I hope to do here – to tell the many stories that reside in these opinions as these stories themselves record (an aspect of) the history of life in American society, all in full awareness that my *own* story (viewpoint and politics) also gets told in the process.

James Clifford made the following point with regard to the difference between history and ethnography. He wrote (1988: 340):

> The distinction between historical and ethnographic practices depends on literate and oral modes of knowledge. History is thought to rest on past – documentary, archival – selections of texts. Ethnography is based on present – oral, experiential, observational – evidence.

The discourse of Supreme Court opinion is a highly literate, written tradition and in this way, it resembles the historical practice that Clifford is writing about. However, there is also an oral aspect to courtroom discourse – the oral exchanges in oral arguments, for example, the private conference meetings that justices hold among themselves, and so on. What I am making a case for here is that we have what looks like a meeting point between historical AND ethnographic practices in so far as judicial discourse is really both oral and written in nature, though the written mode has a way of subsuming, and even silencing, the oral aspects, particularly when justices deliver opinions of the Court with little evidential trace of the other voices (plaintiffs, respondents, other judges, other texts, etc.) that contributed towards the current mode of discourse. In other words, heteroglossia is masked in the monologic nature the judicial opinion takes.

4. Discourse, power and knowledge

In my view, Foucault's emphasis on competing discourses and interacting force relations, vying to produce their own version of knowledge through discursive dominance, is an interesting and a fruitful idea that fits snugly into the ideas of law as a semiotic sign system and that of the discourse-centredness of power relations. Power, according to Foucault, must be understood as "the multiplicity of force relations immanent in the sphere in which they operate and which constitute their own organization" (1978: 92). What this means is that power is not localized at any one point or in any social body, but is a kind of force field. It is much more useful to view power as the interplay of forces in the network. Like the unity of a book that goes "beyond its internal configuration and its autonomous form" and is "caught up in a system of references to other books, other texts, other sentences", each terminal form of power is but "a node within a network" (1972: 23). However, this collaborative power goes beyond the said network of institutions, since there must also be a general consensus coming from below. In other words, the society as a whole is an accomplice in the establishment of power. The complicity alluded to here is similar to Bourdieu's idea of the "doubly determined" nature of symbolic domination (1977: 169). The power that is generated by the convergence of different power terminals and their collaborative acts of conspiracy is then maintained through discourse. Foucault expressed the importance of this discursively maintained power in the following way: "It speaks, and that is the rule" (1978: 83).

Power, viewed as a network of forces, thus yields both positive and negative effects. Power can be repressive in that it can be exercised to exclude and censor. But as Foucault said, "power would be a fragile thing if its only function were to repress" (1980: 59). Instead, power is strong because it is productive in that it generates new knowledge whenever old terms are recast in a new light or when new terms are introduced into the discourse.

In short, for Foucault, discourse is never without a context. No instance of discourse is disembodied discourse for "all manifest discourse is secretly based on an 'already said'" (1972: 25). Every discursive act is therefore "already articulated in the semi-silence that precedes it" (p.25). Hence every text is a response to an on-going dialogue and the process of linguistic negotiation comprises a series of discursive acts that builds on what has gone before. These new discourses are new ways of the articulation of power, and they create what may be seen as new ways of knowing that oppose present and past challenges to power.

Power and knowledge are a kind of "constant articulation" (Foucault 1980: 51) of each other: power creates knowledge; knowledge, manifested in discourse, articulates power. Put another way, it may be said that knowledge and discourse are the resolution of the creative tensions between different levels of power.

Foucault rejected the notion of 'ideology' because it suggests, wrongly for Foucault, that it "stands in virtual opposition to something else which is supposed to count as truth" (1980: 118). In other words, "[p]recisely who manages and intervenes and who is thereby managed is not of importance. . Foucault's 'sovereign' subject is no more than the complex product of colonising discursive knowledge" (Evans 1993: 14). The Foucauldian emphasis, I will again stress, is on the interactional network, not on any singular source of 'truth'.

5. Concluding remarks

I have detailed the nature of my multidisciplinary enterprise and the different strands of ideas that I will employ to tell a story of American life. But for all the "thickness" (Geertz 1973) in the description, the locus must not be lost sight of: language. This stress on language is not because I am primarily a linguist, but for one very important reason: language is not simply the constitutive element in most human activities; it is also the resource (in the sense of capital) used in our construction of worldviews and power as well as the site of consensus and contest. For this reason, whether we speak of political economy or social infrastructure, whether we engage in limitless semiosis or vie for dominance over other groups, the primary means and medium in which all these activities are carried out is language, or as Foucault and Sherzer would have it, discourse. The site of interest is discourse, and the power lies in discourse, and hence the attention must naturally begin with, and be returned, to discourse. In the final analysis, however, I believe the business of language is not the sole property of linguists alone. This is why this study strives to be a cross-disciplinary and multidisciplinary enterprise.

CHAPTER 3

Unequal by law: The early years

> Discourse is the richest point of intersection of the relationship among language, culture, society, and individual expression. In discourse individuals draw on their personal creativity and at the same time on the special and unique resources of the language and culture of their communities, including vocabulary, grammar, norms of interpretation, cultural knowledge and symbolism, systems of genre and style, and rules of effective performance. In so doing, they not only replicate, interpret, and transmit, but actually conceive, create, and recreate their social and cultural reality. . Discourse is the locus of the expression of ideology and especially of the playing out and the working out of conflicts, tensions, and changes inherent in ideological systems.
>
> –Joel Sherzer (1990:6–7)

1. Preliminaries

My data for this chapter consist of excerpts from two United States Supreme Court opinions, *Bradwell v. Illinois (1872)* and *Muller v. Oregon (1908)*. My analysis of these two texts (as with the other two texts in the next chapter) covers lexical choices, grammatical patterning, shifts in meaning (definitions and redefinitions), choice of register and pragmatic power, as well as certain non-linguistic textual features (e.g., judge's style and personality, reliance on precedents, etc.).

I choose as my point of departure the case of *Bradwell v. Illinois (1872)*,[1] a case addressing the issue of a woman's right to an occupation of her choice. The concurring opinion authored by Justice Joseph Bradley (Text 1 in the Appendix) is widely cited by feminist and legal scholars as well as by judges themselves due largely to the extreme conservatism of the views expressed in it. Due to its value as a case that explicitly illustrates the ideology of separate sphere, which characterized much of the nineteenth century in America, *Bradwell* thus serves as a convenient starting point for an understanding of the conservative and traditional background from which the American legal tradition involving gender-related cases has evolved. Text 2 takes us 36 years forward to the case of *Muller v. Oregon (1908)*, in which limitations were placed on the number of hours a woman may be allowed to work outside the home. Both *Bradwell* and *Muller* illustrate the restrictive climate, especially for women, in American law and society in the early years.

This chapter comprises two sections. The first section introduces in greater detail the two cases that generated the two judicial opinions to be discussed here. The second section gives an analysis of the language of the judicial opinions. The point of such a textual analysis is to make an argument for the linguistic indexing of ideology and power at all levels of linguistic structure. Though I will not make the strong claim that any one aspect of language use in the judicial opinion directly points to particular ideologies, I hope to demonstrate, however, that the cumulative effects of the co-occurrence of several types of linguistic usage suggest that a particular kind of ideology and power relations are at play.

2. Background

2.1 An occupation of her choice: The case of Myra Bradwell (1872)

In the history of women's exclusion from the legal profession, the U.S. Supreme Court decision on the case of *Bradwell v. Illinois* is described as a significant step backwards in the pursuit for gender equality (Wohl 2001: 3). Myra Colby Bradwell had studied law under her husband, Judge James Bradwell, and on August 2, 1869, she passed the Illinois bar examination "with high honors" (Friedman 1993: 18). She applied for a licence to practise law in Illinois but obtained the following answer from the Illinois Supreme Court (communication from N.L. Freeman, Illinois Supreme Court reporter, October, 1869, cited in Friedman 1993: 19, emphasis from the original):

> Madam: The court instructs me to inform you that they are compelled to deny your application for a license to practice as an attorney-at-law in the courts of this State, upon the ground that you would not be bound by the [contractual] obligations necessary to be assumed where the relation of attorney and client shall exist, by reason of the DISABILITY IMPOSED BY YOUR MARRIED CONDITION – it being assumed that you are a married woman. . Until such DISABILITY shall be removed by legislation, the court regards itself as powerless to grant your application.

Myra subsequently appealed to the United States Supreme Court. Myra's challenge to the courts, "Does being a woman disqualify [me] under the law of

Illinois from receiving a license to practice law?" (Friedman 1993: 18), was answered with a resounding "Yes" in the Supreme Court's 7–1 decision.[2] In the majority opinion, Justice Miller asserted that:

> [T]here are privileges and immunities belonging to citizens of the United States. .it is these and these alone which a State is forbidden to abridge. But the right to admission to practice in the courts of a State is not one of them.

Justice Joseph Bradley's concurrence, however, situated the Court's judgement on a much broader basis. Citing "the constitution of the family organization" and "divine ordinance", as well as the "destiny and mission of woman", Justice Bradley argued against Myra's right to legal practice based solely on her sex.

The *Bradwell* decision was based squarely on the traditional philosophy of a separate sphere for men and women and the English Common Law notion of "coverture" which essentially suspended the legal status of a married woman, her legal existence being brought under the 'cover' of her husband. The married woman was made completely dependent on her husband for her rights.[3] This doctrine of separate sphere for the sexes required that the public domain be reserved for males and the domestic sphere be the 'proper' place for females (Taub and Schneider 1982).

2.2 In the interest of the race: The case of Mrs Elmer Gotcher (1908)

In 1903, the legislature of the State of Oregon passed the following act (cited in *Muller v. Oregon (1908):* 416):

> That no female (shall) be employed in any mechanical establishment, or factory, or laundry in this State more than ten hours during any one day. The hours of work may be so arranged as to permit the employment of females at any time so that they shall not work more than ten hours during the twenty-four hours of any one day.

In 1908, Curt Muller, who owned a laundry in Portland, Oregon, was convicted and fined $10 under this statute for employing Mrs Elmer Gotcher for more than ten hours a day. Muller appealed to the United States Supreme Court but the Court affirmed the state court's decision "on the grounds that women needed 'special protection' because there was 'something special or different' about them" (Hoff 1991: 197). Text 2 (see the Appendix) is an excerpt of the opinion of the Court delivered by Justice David Brewer.

Like *Bradwell*, the main argument employed in *Muller*, which was also based implicitly on the doctrine of separate spheres for the sexes, was the argument from biology. Unlike *Bradwell,* which stated that "[t]he natural and proper timidity and delicacy which belongs to the female sex evidently unfits it for many of the occupation of civil life" (Text 1), in *Muller*, this reasoning centring on women's presumed physical weakness was more elaborately and explicitly spelt out. As Justice Brewer put it, "[t]hat woman's physical structure and the performance of maternal functions place her at a disadvantage in the struggle for subsistence is obvious" (Text 2). Added to women's presumed physical weakness was women's socially assigned role as "healthy mothers" (Text 2), thus making women's health a public concern in the name of preserving "the strength and vigor of the race" (Text 2). Using these arguments, the Supreme Court in 1908 ruled in favour of limiting the length of time in which a woman could work outside the home.

3. Chains and choices: Gendered discourse, pragmatic power, and judicial rhetoric

3.1 Lexical choices

The kinds of words and phrases that are chosen to make up a stretch of discourse can, on most occasions, betray the views, values and ideology of the speaker or writer. The different ways in which words can be made to mean in varied contexts, whether speakers and writers are conscious of it or not, are the basis of semantic transformations, in which shifts in meaning result in a creation of, as it were, a new universe of discourse, and lexical redefinitions, in which words take on new meanings, and which then give rise to new ways of defining linguistic terms. By studying what individual linguistic items signify or index, and by examining word collocations and co-occurrences in the same text, interesting information may be gathered not just about textual meanings but also about authorial ideological perspectives. The assumptions and presuppositions that lurk behind each of these lexical choices are also examined, for it is in the silences of such unstated assumptions and presuppositions that particular ideologies are articulated.

Following Ochs, the indexing relations, whether direct or indirect, are argued to be the different ways in which gender and power are implicated in the particular choices made at the level of the word. I also argue that the social inequalities in terms of the distribution of power between the two sexes are reflected and affirmed, particularly in these two texts, as is evident from the differing manners in which the male and the female are described. These are taken as indicative of the social and legal ideologies that guided the particular conceptions of gender roles and power structure. The changes that emerge in the later texts (dated 1971 and 1973, see the next chapter) are signalled by the changes in the lexical choices made in them. The general development from a tendency towards essentializing the male to the more clinical attitude towards him in the judicial context should be noted as this gradual change in the Court's preferential attitudes towards the male slowly gave way to more gender equity in more recent decisions.

The *Bradwell* text is noteworthy for its use of the terms "person" and "the sterner sex" (the index and its textual referent are italicised):[4]

> (1) The Supreme Court of Illinois denied the application on the ground that, by the common law, which is the basis of the laws of Illinois, only *men* were admitted to the bar, and the legislature had not made any change in this respect, but had simply provided that no *person* should be admitted to practice as attorney or counsellor without having previously obtained a license for that purpose from two justices of the Supreme Court, and that no *person* should receive a license without first obtaining a certificate from the court of some county of *his* good moral character. (Text 1)

> (2) This fairly belongs to the police power of the State; and, in my opinion, in view of the peculiar characteristics, destiny, and mission of woman, it is within the province of the legislature to ordain what offices, positions, and callings shall be filled and discharged by *men*, and shall receive the benefit of those energies and responsibilities, and that decision and firmness which are presumed to predominate in *the sterner sex.* (Text 1)

In the first example (1), the first appearance of the word "person" in this context may be inferred as directly indexing the male given the legislature has already decreed that *only males* are qualified candidates for admission to the bar.[5] This interpretation receives support from the second use of "person" in the same example (1) as a co-reference of the masculine pronoun, "his". It could of course be argued that "his" may have been used generically in this context, and so does not refer restrictively to the male sex.[6] However, given that females are already excluded in the statement that is made before the point where "his" is used in the text, there is a strong suggestion that this use of "his" does *not* actually carry a generic meaning. Moreover, the rest of the argument in Text 1 supports this interpretation since the female is marked out to be lacking in the necessary degree of "firmness" and "decision" that would qualify her to serve as an attorney. Text 1 also reveals through the use of "the sterner sex" (example 2 above) the first hint of how the male is viewed by the Court, as the 'stronger' sex and hence, he is fitter than the female for certain occupations.

With its use of the phrase "the other sex" to index the male, Text 2 works immediately towards an argument that upholds the separate sphere doctrine:

> (3) Doubtless there are individual exceptions, and there are many respects in which she has an advantage over *him*; but looking at it from the viewpoint of the effort to maintain an independent position in matters from *the other sex*, she is properly placed in a class by herself, and legislation designed for her protection may be sustained, even when like legislation is not necessary for *men* and could not be sustained. (Text 2)

This use of an explicitly exclusionary phrase "the other sex" especially viewed in the light of the judge's characterization in the same context of the female as belonging "in a class by herself" (in example 3 above) serves as a preamble for an elaboration of the argument for the separateness between the sexes that is to come later in the text:

> (4) The two sexes differ in structure of body, in the functions to be performed by each, in the amount of physical strength, in the capacity for long-continued labor, particularly when done standing, the influence of vigorous health upon the future well-being of the race, the self-reliance which enables one to assert full rights, and in the capacity to maintain the struggle for subsistence (Text 2).

> (5) This difference justifies a difference in legislation and upholds that which is designed to compensate for some of the burdens which rest upon her. . (Text 2)

Indirect indexical relations are expected to be more prevalent in any one text than direct indexical relations (Ochs 1992). This is true of the two texts studied here as most of the lexical items that refer to the male are found not to index gender directly but index the social roles and activities of the male. For example, the social role of the male is defined as "husband" to the female and he acts as "her head and representative in the social state" (Text 1). As is also explicitly stated in the text,

> (6) Man is, and should be, *woman's protector and defender* (Text 1).

In addition, the male is socially admired and deemed to be suitable for his role as legal counsellors, especially when he possesses both "good moral character" and "skill and confidence" (Text 1). Having these attributes, the activities of the male are overtly associated with the public domain of legal office, and his capabilities are said to contribute to the "proper administration of justice" (Text 1). Text 1 is particularly rich in lexical items that show the indexing of male roles and activities and the social ascription of male attributes.

Text 2 is very similar to Text 1 with regard to the use of indirect indexicals to describe the social roles, activities and attributes of the male in the society. In this text, the male stance in relation to the female is designated either as "brother" or "employer". For example, the Court asserted that:

> (7) It is impossible to close one's eyes to the fact that she still looks to *her brother* and depends upon him (Text 2).

The male whose "superior physical strength" makes him dependable is then argued to exert 'legitimate' "control" over the female. The Court stated in this respect that:

> (8) *He* established *his control* at the outset by *superior physical strength*, and *this control in various forms*, with diminishing intensity, has continued to the present (Text 2).

However, the male in Text 2 is also recognized as flawed in that he is filled with "greed" and "passion", which provides the Court, curiously enough, with another reason, *not* to restrain the male but to 'protect' the female instead. The underlying belief that the female should be protected (thus naturalizing her helplessness and vulnerability) rather than the male be restrained (hence, naturalizing male passions) is reflected in the path in which the Court chooses to take. The socially ascribed attributes of the male are thus argued to make him more adept in the "struggle for subsistence" (Text 2), whereas his flaws are reasons for the special protection of women via the limit that must be imposed on the number of hours that they are permitted to work in the public sphere.

These two texts display some rather interesting lexical terms that index the female. Special mention should be given to the use of "it" and "minors" in Text 1 and Text 2 respectively:

> (9) The natural and proper timidity and delicacy which belongs to *the female sex* evidently unfits *it* for many of the occupations of civil life (Text 1).
>
> (10) As *minors*, though not to the same extent, *she* has been looked upon in the courts as needing especial care that her rights may be preserved (Text 2).

It seems puzzling but definitely revealing that the Court chooses to refer to the female sex not as "woman" or "her" but as "it" in Text 1, especially when one recalls that the male sex, referred in Texts 1 and 2 as respectively "the sterner sex" or "the other sex", has been consistently marked out as "men" or "him," as follows:

> (11) This fairly belongs to the police power of the State; and, in my opinion, in view of the peculiar characteristics, destiny, and mission of woman, it is within the province of the legislature to ordain what offices, positions, and callings shall be filled and discharged by *men* and shall receive the benefit of those energies and responsibilities, and that decision and firmness which are presumed to predominate in *the sterner sex* (Text 1).

> (12) Doubtless there are individual exceptions, and there are many respects in which she has an advantage over *him*, but looking at it from the viewpoint of the effort to maintain an independent position in matters from *the other sex*, she is properly placed in a class by herself, and legislation designed for her protection may be sustained, even when like legislation is not necessary for *men* and could not be sustained (Text 2).

Though it may be argued that the use of "the female *sex*" rather than "the female" to some extent might have favoured the use of "it" rather than "her", I argue that the use of an inanimate pronoun to index the female sex directly, especially in the absence of such a parallel indexing of the male sex, reveals an imbalance of treatment of the sexes in the law. The use of the inanimate pronoun "it" seems also to index grammatically woman's socially and legally ascribed physical weakness, rendering her literally incapable and incompetent to assert her right to legal practice in the context of *Bradwell.*

In Text 2, the female is placed in the same category as "minors". While the principle of coverture leaves the married woman dependent on her husband, the equation of women with minors renders the dependency complete. The effect of the collapse of the lexico-semantic fields of "woman" and "minor" is to further restrict the rights of the female in the same way that children do not enjoy the same rights as adults. The classification of woman with minors thus furnishes the ground for the Court's and society's enforced protection of the female in the name of "especial care" (Text 2) due to her helpless state, thus leading up to restrictive legislative measures said to be designed to 'protect' and preserve her rights.

Turning to the indirect indexing of female social roles, activities and attributes, the argument in Text 1 emphasizes woman's marital status. As a reading of Text 1 will attest, whether married or unmarried, the female in the Bradley opinion has no place in the public domain. If married, she is incapacitated by the "complications" arising from the married state due to the doctrine of coverture, her rights being brought under the auspices of her husband. If unmarried, she is still dismissed as an anomalous exception to "the general rule" as Justice Bradley made explicit:

> (13) a woman had no legal existence separate from her husband. .many of the special rules of law flowing from and dependent upon this cardinal principle still exist in full force in most States. One of these is, that the married woman is incapable, without her husband's consent, of making contracts which shall be binding on her or him. This very incapacity was one circumstance which the Supreme Court of Illinois deemed important in rendering the married woman incompetent fully to perform the duties and trusts that belong to the office of any attorney or counsellor. It is true that many women are unmarried and not affected by any of the duties, complications, and incapacities arising out of the married state but these are exceptions to the general rule. . And the rules of civil society must be adapted to the general constitution of things and cannot be based upon exceptional cases (Text 1).

In short, the female cannot be accommodated by law under both circumstances. The only accommodation given her is the construction that she is 'not male' and even, 'not adult' (Text 2) and these are categories that are laden with dire consequences during the times of *Bradwell* and *Muller.*

In addition to her role as "wife", the woman is also consigned to the role of "mother", these two roles being her "paramount destiny and mission" (Text 1) in life. Furthermore, the female is said not only to be naturally and properly timid and delicate, but she is also endowed with "peculiar characteristics" (Text 1), all presumably not suitable for public life. Given these incapacities, her participation in civil life is reduced to a "privilege" as opposed to a full-fledged right of citizenship (Text 1). The inherent weaknesses of character and nature that have caused woman's exclusion from public office, however, are apparently not serious enough that she cannot play an important role in the domestic sphere. The private domain is hence her 'proper' place where the female activities of mothering and overseeing the home are to be dutifully enacted and legally sanctioned. The roles, attributes and activities that are associated with the female are thus clearly spelt out in Text 1.

Text 2 is remarkably similar to Text 1 with regard to the nature of the indirect indexical relations that are present to define the woman and her domain. The opening statement in Text 2 serves as a strong statement of the assumption that guides the Court's argument for enforcing the special protection of women:

> (14) That woman's physical structure and the performance of maternal functions place her at a disadvantage in the struggle for subsistence is obvious.

Endowed with a weak "physical structure" which makes a woman prone to "injurious effects" if she were to be allowed to engage in "long-continued labor", the female is said to be suitable for roles (such as, being a mother) specially tailored to "her disposition" (Text 2). It is especially interesting to note that the ill-effects of "long-continued labor" applies only to work in the *public* domains and does not seem to extend to women's work within the *home*, which, for many women at that time, is a full-time obligation. Hence, the 'rightful' place of the woman is once again defined as the home, where she stands alone in "a class by herself" (Text 2). While the weakness of the female constitution calls for legal protection, her duty towards preserving "the strength and vigor of the race" justifies elevating the concern for her health to a matter of "public interest and care" (Text 2). In this manner of characterization, the female not only has no voice concerning how long she can labour outside the home, but more importantly perhaps, she does not even have jurisdiction over her own health as it is now relegated to a social and public concern, and thus has become a property of the State.[7] The indexing of female roles and activities in Text 2, therefore, pronounces far-reaching consequences for women.

3.2 Grammatical patterning

An analysis of three aspects of grammar – subject-verb predication, mood choice, and modality – will show the differences in the power that is commanded by the Courts and by other sources of authority (divine, medical, historical, etc.) on the one hand, and the general lack of power exhibited by the layperson standing before the Court on the other. The selection of three aspects of grammatical patterning amply illustrates my point that the power difference between judges and laypersons, and the inequalities between men and women, are inscribed in the grammar of judicial discourse. In addition, by looking at different strands of grammatical patterning, I also show that imbalances of power and status are constituted by more than a single grammatical dimension. Hence, the analysis of mood enriches and supplements the examination of the subject-verb predication, for example, in a way which demonstrates that power and inequalities in discourse are distributed throughout the system of grammar, and not in any one dimension alone. Since specific ideologies are expressed by specific choices of grammatical resources, my concentration on three separate but related strands of grammatical patterning will show the pervasiveness of inequalities, ideology and power. Finally, I have chosen to pay particular attention to these three aspects because they are sensitive indicators on issues of power. As I will argue, the predication of grammatical subjects indexing different sources of authority (e.g., "the Court") with performative verbs (e.g., "order") is not an accident of grammar, but is a textual reflection of the concentration of power in select camps. Similarly, the judicial choice of the declarative mood and the use of certain modals to express moral and legal imperatives are grammatical contributions to the construction of power and ideology in judicial discourse. I stress, however, that my selective analysis of predication, mood, and modals is meant only to show how certain aspects of the grammar inscribe and constitute particular ideologies, and hence, in no way am I saying that these are the only features in the grammar that are worthy of attention.

3.2.1 *Subject-verb predication*

Two kinds of subject-verb predication are salient in the judicial texts I have examined. The first set of grammatical subjects and verbs denotes the semantic field that is characterized by the presence of power, i.e. the grammatical subjects in this set (such as, "the Court") index referents which have access to power and authority. These 'powerful' grammatical subjects are predicated in judicial discourse with a special class of verbs, called performative verbs or verbs of 'saying' (such as, "to question"), and these verbs describe the kind of speech acts that the sources of authority perform. In contrast, the second set of grammatical subjects and verbs occupies the semantic field where little power is available to the actors. The referents indexed by these grammatical subjects (such as, "the plaintiff") and the actions described by predominantly material and relational verbs (e.g., "is") that are predicated to them do not display the power and authority that are clearly evident in the first set.[8] I argue that this difference in the grammatical patterning is a textual indexing of the differences in power between the authoritative officers of the Court and the powerless laypersons standing before it. It should be noted that regardless of the individual character of each of the two judicial texts under study here, they exhibit the same tendency, showing two groups of grammatical subjects and their corresponding verbs.

First, attention is directed to the nature of the sources of authority in the two texts. The following examples are representative in terms of their continual occurrence in judicial discourse, though exactly which kind of authority is invoked in each case may differ from text to text, and from era to era. Some examples are:

Table 1. Sources of authority

Type of authority	Text 1	Text 2
LAW	the judgment of the court, fourteenth amendment of the Constitution	the courts, statutes
GOVERNMENT	the legislature	legislation
HISTORY/TRADITION	historical fact, time immemorial	history
NATURE/DESTINY	nature, destiny	–
RELIGION	divine ordinance, the law of the Creator	–
		–
VALUES	family institution	–
RULES	general rule, cardinal principle	–
REASON	reason, ground	–
MEDICINE	–	medical fraternity
UTILITARIANISM	–	well-being of the race, benefit of all
FACT/TRUTH	–	fact

Table 1 captures the nature and the range of authority that are invoked in the two judicial opinions. These authoritative sources range from law to history to truth. The web of meanings created by this appeal to specific authorities reveals a rather interesting type of ideological orientation that is reminiscent of Enlightenment rationalism. It is clear that a particular kind of knowledge construction is in place.

The above patterning also shows the development in the choice of authoritative sources that the different courts accept as legitimate sources of appeal to support the legal arguments used in each opinion. For example, religion and tradition were accepted as legitimate voices of appeal, as their occurrences in Texts 1 and 2 show. More recent judicial opinions do not appeal to any of these sources of authority. Instead, as will be evident, there seems to be a shift towards an appeal to the scope of rights and specific legal principles. Another point of interest in the later texts is the focus on the meanings of specific stretches of language, underscoring the linguistic nature of law and the reliance on linguistic meanings and definitions in the judicial setting. Such a shift creates new webs of meaning that help to effect new directions in the manner in which the opinions of the Court take.

Sometimes, instead of "This Court", "we" is used in the text when the Court refers to itself. The pronoun "we", when used in this judicial context, does not necessarily refer to a clear majority. Thus the use of "we" projects a false unity that glosses over the underlying judicial disagreements, creating the semblance of a seamless discourse undisrupted or unfragmented by voices of dissent. The heteroglossia that characterises the process of judicial decision-making is thus silenced and homogenised into a monologic opinion fronted by one judge or a group of judges. This reveals a separate dimension of power and power struggles within the Court itself.

However, if the use of "we" has the effect of silencing the voices of disagreements, by the same token, the vagueness denoted by "we" serves also as a protective cover, in which no one justice of the Court may be subjected to challenge, since not one, but a whole group, is indexed by its use. Hence the unanimity, or in some cases, the majority view that is projected by "we" effects an institutional force and unity, which protects even when it silences individual judges, particularly the ones whose opinions depart from the majority vote.

Whatever the sources of authority, however, the power that is indexed by any of the above terms is immense, for every invocation of any of the sources of authority carries with it the sense of an already pre-established legitimacy that has full institutional and social recognition. In Foucauldian terms, the Court's invocation of, say science, as an authoritative voice has the effect of mobilizing an entire set of scientific knowledge that enables the Court to reason its way to some desired conclusion. In such an instance, the Court's power, in combination with the scientific forces that are appealed to, are marshalled against or for the plaintiff or state as the case may be towards a judicial resolution of a particular issue.

The power of institution appears even more discernible when we note the verbs that collocate with these grammatical subjects. Table 2 below gives a selection of verbs (with their grammatical or logical subjects) used in the two texts:

Table 2. Some examples of grammatical subjects and verbs indexing power.

Text	Subject	Verb
1	The Supreme Court of Illinois	denied
	The legislature	ordains
	The legislature	had intended
	Statute	excluded (by)
	The civil law	has (always) recognized
	The fourteenth amendment of the Constitution	declares
2	History	discloses
	legislation	removed (by)
	some legislations	(to) protect
	he	established
	legislation	removed (by)

Table 2 shows what the different sources of authority can or cannot do, whether it is to deny a petition, ordain or put into force certain rules, or to remove a restriction. It is easily discernible from the table above that the occurrences within Texts 1 and 2 of authoritative subjects accompanied by verbs denoting powerful acts are quite prevalent in these texts. Two points of interest may be noted from this subject-verb list. First, the images conjured up by these verbs are suggestive of the extensive arm of the law and the other authorities. Just as in religious contexts where God is said to ordain X or Y, the legislature is said to have the power "to *ordain* what offices, positions, and callings shall be filled and discharged by men" (Text 1). The power of the legislature to specify who is a suitable candidate for a certain position is constructed as an unchallengeable stance. Similarly, like a father in a patriarchal order, the legislature and some laws are said to 'protect' women from society's ills, thus testifying to the patriarchal belief that is in place then:

> (15) She will still be where some legislation *to protect* her seems necessary to secure a real equality of right (Text 2).

What I have just observed is the varied but always powerful and definitive manners in which the Court or justices can act, and must act, vested as they are with institutional powers of office. As Bourdieu has said in connection with the "rites of institution" (1982b: 121):

> The authorized spokesperson is the one whom it behoves and on whom it is incumbent to speak on behalf of the collectivity. It is both his privilege and his

> duty, his proper function, in a word, his competence (in the legal sense of the term).

Hence, judges are authorized to speak and write in the powerful ways that they do. This is their judicial privilege. It is also their judicial duty that causes judges to speak and write in the ways that I am noting here; otherwise they will not be recognized as acting 'properly' in the way judges are required to act.

A second point of interest about these verbs is that most of them may be said to be performative verbs, encapsulating what authorities can do simply through the act of saying, thus providing excellent exemplifications of 'the power of the word' or speech acts. Witness, for instance, the following:

> (16) The Supreme Court of Illinois *denied* the application. .(Text 1).[9]

The Court can thus deny certain requests and, on many occasions, will explain certain rules that apply to the case. Inanimate rules of law are endowed with the power of speech. A particular amendment is given a life of its own and described as 'declaring' what is within legal limits:

> (17) . . *the fourteenth amendment of the Constitution*, which *declares* that no State shall make or enforce any law which shall abridge the privileges and immunities of citizens of the United States. .(Text 1).

This way of making laws speak in place of judges also has a way of shielding individual judges behind the faceless power of institution as instanced by, say, the Fourteenth Amendment. Such a conventional feature of legal discourse is normally assumed to be non-significant – this is a view that I am arguing against here.

The verbs used in the above context thus reflect the immense amount of power that judges, courts, and laws (and other authoritative sources) have at their disposal. These verbs not only describe what the agents are doing, but their use also realizes the very actions they describe through a mere pronouncement (in the appropriate context). These verbs may thus be called performative verbs in the sense used by Austin (1962) and Searle (1969), although some of them, while not performative verbs in themselves, behave remarkably like performative verbs in the context of judicial performance. Whether it is to deny or to affirm, to forbid or to establish, these verbs require that the agent stand in a position of authority. The speaker says it, and it is so. It is the presence of these performative and performative-like verbs in the judicial opinions that constitutes judicial discourse as social action. This quality is responsible, in part at least, for the impression that judicial discourse exudes immense power and authority.

In contrast to the patterning of grammatical subjects denoting authority with performative verbs and verbs of 'saying', there exists another type of subject-verb patterning in these two judicial texts, which index very little power, if any at all. Table 3 below is a selection to illustrate this pattern:

Table 3. Some examples of grammatical subjects and verbs indexing powerless referents

Text	Subject	Verb
1	Women	engage
	Man	is
	The claim of the plaintiff	is
	This very incapacity	was
2	They	are (not)
	The burdens of motherhood	are
	Woman	has been
	She	shall labor

The contrast between Table 2 and Table 3 is clearly discernible. One of the more specific subject reference found in Text 1 is "the plaintiff". Most of the other references are phrases like "a woman", "every citizen", "he" or "she", and "appellant" or "appellee". In other words, most of the grammatical subjects are unspecific and sometimes vague, and if specific, the referents denoted lone persons who are clearly not in a position of power. Though it may be argued that "this Court" is to some extent also a vague reference, it is nevertheless more specific in that it refers *situationally* to an elite group and its position in a legal order and process and it certainly carries with it much more power than something like "a woman" or "the appellant". Moreover, an important difference between "this Court" and "the plaintiff" is that the former connotes an institutional unity while the latter refers to a lone individual with little backing (contrast the earlier discussion of "we"). It is clear that the potential referents indexed by the grammatical subjects such as the ones in Table 3 differ markedly with regard to their access to power by virtue of their individual and socially defined roles as justice seekers. In a web of meaning, this group of agents constitutes a universe of individuals that lies outside the elite circle, and thus, by its very nature, has little access to resources and power, and hence by such a lack of access, whatever discourse is generated by this group is not likely to constitute new modes of knowledge construction.

The verbs that accompany these 'weak' grammatical subjects are found to be predominantly material (i.e. action-based) and relational (indicating relationships) in nature, with fewer performative-type verbs occurring in this context. With an absence of such verbs that denote speech and its attendant power, it is not a big surprise that no new knowledge may be generated in this realm, or if generated, such knowledge is not likely to be established as dominant in any way. The only isolated instances of verbs approximating to the performative category turn out to be verbs such as "conceded" and "argue", these having little to do with power (at least not in the performative sense) on the part of the agents, as is clear from their meanings. Instead, these verbs express the burdens placed on these subjects to persuade and convince the Court of one way of reasoning rather than another, and in failing to do so, they must concede their point and in many cases, admit defeat. In other words, these agents cannot merely assert their power in the way that authoritative entities can; they have to establish their own mode of reasoning, and on failing, must surrender their causes. There is, in short, little power from these positions of burden.

Relational verbs express relationships, and examples taken from the texts include "belongs", "became", and the forms of the verbs "be" and "has" ("is", "are", "was", "have" etc). In Text 1, for instance, it was said that

> (18) The paramount destiny and mission of woman *are* to fulfill the noble and benign offices of wife and mother. This *is* the law of the Creator.

In Text 2, the following is taken as an obvious fact:

> (19) That woman's physical structure and the performance of maternal functions place her at a disadvantage in the struggle for subsistence *is* obvious.

When two distinct propositions are linked by relational verbs such as these, the effect that is created is one of a mapping of two sets of realities into a natural fit. Whether it is the case of an "X is Y" or "X belongs to Y" or to put it differently, "Y has X", the fact that the two distinct propositions or entities are placed within the text in such close proximity and then linked by a relationship of identity ("is"), possession or ownership ("has") or belonging ("belongs") makes it easy to treat the two *as if* they are one and the same (or similar at least). A kind of necessary and naturalized connection is thus created through such grammatical constructions of associative relations, where one may not logically or empirically exist. In the present context, the consequence of bringing into existence certain relationships is such that women are perceived as naturally weak and as naturally suited for their roles in the private sphere, thus legitimizing the arguments subsequently made in favour of women's exclusion in public life. That a linguistic connection could effect such dire social consequences (here, literally sealing women's fate); that language can be used to effect the rationalization of such a socio-cultural ideology is, to say the least, a testament of the power of language to innovate, maintain and perpetuate dominant ideologies and viewpoints.

Previous research has attested that powerless language is not the sole property of women *per se*, but that powerless language will be found where there are individuals, whether male or female, who find themselves, for whatever reason located in a position that lacks power (O'Barr and Atkins 1980). Added to this is Conley and O'Barr's (1990) finding in small claims courts that most judges tend to adopt a rule-oriented style in presiding over cases whereas most laypersons tend to treat the legal setting relationally, i.e., as a means to resolve personal misunderstandings and to mend frayed relationships. While this trend is not absolute (since there are both relational judges and rule-oriented plaintiffs and defendants, and some individuals, on occasions, adopt a combination of styles), the tendency that is noted here seems accurate for the most part. In this regard then, the association of performative and performative-type verbs with the grammatical subjects denoting authority and the association of relational verbs with the grammatical subjects indexing little power become significant. Performative verbs may be argued to be rule-oriented verbs since these are the verbs that dictate the denial of rights and the establishment of laws. Relational verbs, on the other hand, express relations between entities. The powerful and powerless positions evident in the two texts correlate with instances of performative acts and relational processes respectively. Though women are not the sole users of powerless language, it is nevertheless the case that women tend to be found in positions with less power and, thus, they tend to employ less powerful language. The patterning of relational processes with powerless grammatical subjects may then be said to signal a *feminization* of the powerless position of plaintiffs and respondents (both male and female).

3.2.2 Mood choice

The importance of mood choice in discourse lies in the information the particular choice can yield in terms of the adopted stance of the speaker or writer. The mood system is an expression of the particular "speech role" that speakers or writers adopt in their discourse (Halliday 1985:68ff). When one asks a question, one adopts the role of an information seeker; when one makes a statement, one becomes the supplier of information.

The following are some clauses drawn from the two texts under study here. In each clause, the declarative mood structure, subject [-wh] + finite ordering, i.e., a non-wh word subject followed by a finite verb, is observed:

> (20) *The court*, however, *regarded* itself as bound by at least two limitations. (Text 1)
>
> (21) *Man is*, and *should be*, woman's protector and defender. (Text 1)
>
> (22) *She will* still be where some legislation to protect her seems necessary to secure a real equality of right. (Text 2)

The significance of using statements to cast the judicial opinion seems to be a function of the judicial situation, the role of judges, and the nature of judicial discourse itself. Judicial opinions, especially Supreme Court opinions, are the final rulings of judges presiding in the Courts. As such, it is expected that the decisions that are handed down will convey not a simple 'opinion' of the Court but will carry with it the full powers with which a high Court is entrusted. As a result, the tone of the Court will be expected, and this is in fact the case here, to be one of absolute authority. In order to convey its power and legitimacy, the choice of the declarative mood becomes especially appropriate since the ultimate business of the Court is not to ask questions (not at this decision-making stage anyway, except perhaps rhetorical ones), but to declare (in the performative sense of a declaration) its decision on any given matter. And not only does the Court have to provide statements about the nature of its decision, it also has to state its case in a manner that is consistent with its authority. These considerations, therefore, dictate the choice of the declarative mood – the primary mood to make assertions and to characterize statements *as if* they are facts.

There is, however, another important effect of the use of the declarative mood in judicial texts – it provides a masking effect that is crucial to maintaining and upholding the Court's authority. Even when the Court's rulings are stated with factual authority, it is still undeniable that even the most solidly grounded rules are grounded only in the Court's own domain. In other words, the Court's pronouncements are only respected if the whole institutional set-up of the legal system is upheld as valid for the society in question. As long as the legal institution remains only an aspect (among many) of the social arrangements that individuals in the society have agreed to recognize as a legitimate source of authority, it cannot avoid recognizing that it is, at its base, a purely social construction. The statements that the Court issues are thus, at best, socially constructed 'facts' that happened to be socially recognized as such. The validity of the Court is therefore both conveyed by and perpetuated through the use of the declarative mood.

Another function served by the declarative mood in the judicial setting is that the assertions effect a judicial monologue carrying the voice of a solitary speaker or writer. Statements of 'facts' require no corresponding response, in contrast to any normal adjacency pairs.[10] There is thus no genuine dialogue (in the sense of a two-way verbal encounter or social exchange between the judge and, say, the plaintiff) in these judicial texts even when these texts may be said to be rooted in some prior initiation or provocation from outside the legal system. Hence, though two sets of participants are reflected in the judicial opinions (as my subject-verb analysis shows) there exists only one voice in the texts – that of the judicial speaker/author, speaking and writing on behalf of the Court. However, the implicit understanding that operates in judicial discourse is that the Court's statements are directed at the individuals most closely connected with the case at hand and to the society at large, and thus there is an audience 'out there' who is being spoken to. Yet, the monologic nature of these statements does not allow for a more active interaction between the parties. Hill's (1985: 729) interpretation of Bakhtin's view on the effect of the monologic style is that the monologue "permits no challenge" and it yields the point of view of a single voice that is "ideologically consisten[t]" (Bakhtin 1929).

The choice of the declarative mood serves, then, to reinforce the legitimacy and finality of the Court's decision, and consequently it serves as a multiple index of (1) the Court's standing as authority, (2) the Court's role as the final arbiter of 'truth' and justice, appointed to make certain pronouncements, (3) the performative function of the Court in executing various performative acts, and (4) the activities of the Court in terms of its capacity as law-giver and law-keeper.

3.2.3 Modality

The expression of modal meanings in the judicial texts serves to reinforce the legal and moral power of the Court. Traditional studies of English modals (Palmer 1986, 1990) differentiate between two main uses of modals – namely, an epistemic use and a deontic use. Epistemic modality ("modes of knowing") expresses judgements and opinions arrived at from knowledge of prevailing circumstances; deontic modality (or "modes of obligation") expresses "what is obligatory, permitted or forbidden" (Palmer 1990: 7). Epistemic modality is, hence, an expression of the degrees of certainty and possibility in which an event will occur, whereas, deontic modality "is tied in with all sorts of social knowledge: the speaker's belief systems about morality and legality; and her estimations of power and authority" (Saeed 1997: 127).

Eve Sweetser (1990) argues that there are good historical and socio-linguistic reasons "for viewing the epistemic use of modals as an extension of a more basic root [i.e., deontic] meaning" (p.50). Sweetser's basic argument is that modals do not have two distinct types of uses and meanings (the traditional epistemic v. deontic contrast) but that the two meanings are related in a systematic way. Sweetser maintains that the historical development of modal meanings has proceeded from a purely non-modal usage denoting a kind of force, to the root/deontic meaning, and finally to the epistemic use (p.50).[11] In such an extension from the deontic to the epistemic, the mental structures of reasonings (deontic) and the physical world of actions (epistemic), are mapped onto each other. Thus, epistemic uses of modals are argued to have originated from the deontic uses, and not vice versa.

Whether an epistemic or deontic use of modals is employed in the judicial texts, the authority of the Court is still preserved. The difference lies in the *basis* (whether moral reasoning, epistemic inevitability or factual grounds) in which authority is invoked. The use of modals in the judicial context thus creates, or appears to create, a sense of inevitability and an aura of authority. My claim is that given the nature of the judicial setting, modal usage that is laden with deontic meaning serves to enhance judicial power even more. It is found that in both the *Bradwell* and the *Muller* texts, more than 50% of the modals are used to express the Court's imposed restrictions, or the Court's dictates of what action is or is not permissible. The following is a breakdown of the modal occurrences expressing deontic meaning used in the two texts.

Table 4. Use of modals in *Bradwell* and *Muller*

	should	shall	can	may	will	must
TEXT 1	7	5	3	0	0	1
TEXT 2	0	1	2	3	3	0

Text 1 has a high number of *should* and *shall*. These are said to express the speaker's responsibility to achieve some action (Sweetser 1990). In this context, the law imposes restrictions and the Court pronounces what should be the case. The high number of *should* (7 occurrences) coincides with the more overtly dictatorial and prescriptive attitude adopted by Justice Bradley in Text 1 and is consistent with the paternalistic stance taken by earlier courts. An example of such a use of *should* follows:

(23) Man is, and *should* be, woman's protector and defender (Text 1).

Clearly, it is the obligation of the male to protect the female and the Court is unambiguous in its affirmation of such a state of affair. Similarly, the use of *must*, though sparingly in these excerpts, occurs in all texts (see the next chapter for discussion of the other two texts) except for Text 2. *must* expresses the moral and legal obligation that the judicial speaker pronounces on its audience. These three modals, *should*, *shall*, and *must*, thus express "moral obligation, or duty (defined in moral or legal terms)" (Coates 1983: 59, 185).

Can(not) is found in both texts whereas *may* is found in all texts (see next chapter) but absent in Text 1. The overlapping semantics between one possible meaning of *can* and the semantics of *may* have been noted before (for example, "I can go" v. "You may go," see Sweetser 1990: 52ff). Sweetser defines the relatedness of *can* and *may* as a question of a "positive ability on the part of the doer" (*can*) and a "lack of restriction on the part of someone else" (*may*). Given these definitions, I interpret the use of these particular modals in the judicial context as denoting both the power (*can*) and the limits (*cannot*) of the Court or the law as well as denoting the Court's roles in granting permission or lifting restrictions (*may*). More will be said about the use of *may* when I discuss the *Roe* text. Suffice it to say that in all these usages, the power of the Court, as exercised through its interpretation of laws is immense (even though there are certain constraints): what one is entitled to as an individual has to be achieved through the Court's particular interpretations of specific laws, and similarly, what one cannot do is something that is defined by a different set of judicial interpretation. In other words, officers of the Court, as legal interpreters, are the givers and the takers of rights.

Finally, *will* expresses a prediction of the inevitable. Text 2, in particular, stresses the disadvantages that women will incur if they were not specially protected by law:

> (24) Though limitations upon personal and contractual rights may be removed by legislation, there is that in her disposition and habits of life which *will* operate against a full assertion of those rights.

Women's physical frailty is said to contribute to their inability to exercise their rights to the fullest, and this 'fact' is then said to cause women's inherent dependency on men, thus creating the 'natural' need for protective legislation.

The judicial opinions I examine also show the presence of non-modal lexical items that clearly also index the power and authority of the Court. An example from Text 1 is:

> (25) In view of this latter limitation the court felt *compelled* to deny the application of females to be admitted as members of the bar.

Because the form "compelled to deny" can be transformed into an equivalent modal usage "*must* deny", it can be argued that this form, though 'de-modalized', still expresses the same force that modals express. It is further noted that the above structure is an agentless-passive, where the actor compelling the court to act in ways unfavourable to Myra Bradwell is left indeterminate. The use of such forms in the judicial texts thus enhances the power inherent in the discourse that is examined here.

Given the meanings that are conveyed by these uses of modal expressions in the judicial text, it is clearly discernible that power is concentrated in one party: the Court. Through expressions of modality, and reinforced by the declarative mood, the Court asserts its legal authority, constantly dictating what those bound by the rule of law are permitted (or not permitted) to do. Even when the rights of individuals are discussed, the apportionment and ascription of these rights are still determined by the Court and by its interpretation of the law.

3.3 Shifts in meaning

It is possible to identify certain types or styles of arguments that may bias the judicial decision in one direction rather than another. Each of these arguments may be shown to be based in a very important way on the manner in which certain lexical items are assigned meaning. I will discuss the semantics of the terms "person", "sphere", "destiny", and "administration of justice" as they occur in the judicial texts for various reasons. First, in their own ways, these terms have bearings on the question of gender, and the changes in their semantics are of direct relevance to the issue of discursive shifts. Second, there are far-reaching legal consequences that result from the determination of the meaning of these terms and this is relevant to an understanding of the process of change and evolution with regard to gender justice in American law and society. Third, the determination of meaning is an act of authorial power manifested in discourse, and a study of such a display of power will further enrich my description of the indexing of power and ideology in the judicial texts.

First, the issue of personhood. In Text 1, the definition of the term "person" may be argued to be one of the key issues that decides the case against granting a woman the right to the choice of an occupation. As Text 1 shows, the judge began with seemingly gender-neutral lexical choices such as "attorney" or "counsellor-at-law" and "person" which when viewed in the context of their use may be read as referring to both males and females:

> (26) The claim of the plaintiff, who is a married woman, to be admitted to practice as *an attorney and counsellor-at-law*, is based upon the supposed right of *every person, man or woman*, to engage in any lawful employment for a livelihood. The Supreme Court of Illinois denied the application on the ground that, by the common law, which is the basis of the laws of Illinois, *only men were admitted to the bar*, and the legislature had not made any change in this respect, but had simply provided that *no person should be admitted to practice as attorney or counsellor* without having previously obtained a license for that purpose from two justices of the Supreme Court, and that *no person* should receive a license without first obtaining a certificate from the court of some county of *his* good moral character.

However, the situation changes swiftly from this point onwards when Justice Bradley reaffirmed the laws of Illinois that determined that "only men were [to be] admitted to the bar". If only males were intended by the legislature as suitable candidates for legal office, and if the application by females was to be denied by law, then "counsellor" and "person", words that are gender-neutral and all-inclusive in theory, when used in the context just mentioned, exclusively index *only* the male in practice.

The choice of such 'neutral' vocabulary is important for two reasons. First, it makes the law appear neutral and objective, reinforcing the law's image of fairness with respect to all citizens. Second, the subtle shifts in the meaning of these so-called all-inclusive terms will go largely unnoticed if readers do not pay close attention to how these terms are used in the text. One can note the very subtle slippage from "every person, man or woman", which denotes a specific, clearly bounded set of meaning, to "persons, not intended by the legislature to be admitted", where here, there is an immediate narrowing of the web of meaning first established, OR the shift from the use of "attorney" to refer to any qualified individual to the use of the same term which excludes women on the grounds that women are "incompetent" to fulfill the "duties and trusts that belong to the office of any attorney or counsellor" (Text 1). In short, the restriction of the meaning of 'personhood' in this case rules out the participation of females in public life, as one set of meaning is substituted by another smaller and more restrictive set of meaning.

I turn next to the semantics of "spheres" and "destinies". In Text 1, the phrase "the respective spheres and destinies of man and woman" is initially used when Justice Bradley spoke about the wide differences in the roles and domains of males and females. This usage merely acknowledges that the "spheres" and "destinies" of the two sexes are different from one another, and that both males and females have their own spheres of operation, with certain destinies to fulfill. However, Justice Bradley continued in his opinion to associate "spheres" and "destinies" only with women:

> (27) The constitution of the family organization, which is founded in the divine ordinance, as well as in the nature of things, indicates *the domestic sphere* as that which *properly belongs to the domain and functions of womanhood. . The paramount destiny and mission of woman* are to fulfill the noble and benign offices of wife and mother.

While the opinion earlier states that *both* sexes have their own destinies and occupy their own spheres, later remarks involving the subjects of "spheres" and "destinies" are abruptly shifted in the discourse from a more inclusive meaning to one that is clearly restricted to and associated with *women only*. In contrast, not a single use of "destiny", "mission", or "sphere" is employed in relation to the specifications of male roles and domains. Instead, male roles are ennobled and cast within the semantics of "duties and trusts" as well as "callings" and "responsibilities". The alignment between the domestic sphere and the female role, and the dissociation of the private domain of the home from the male role, as if the male has no important role to play in the home, constitute a drastic relocation of the semantics of both "spheres" and "destiny". In this circular manner of defining these terms, the doctrine of separate spheres is maintained. The collapse in the meaning potential of particular lexical items, in terms of how narrower associations between particular lexis and their meanings are built into the terms in these texts, therefore, are crucial in shaping the arguments in a discourse that worked towards restricting the rights of one set of individuals.

Just as the range of associative meanings can be collapsed in the course of one text, the reverse phenomenon, the expansion of semantic range, is also discernible. In Text 1, after Justice Bradley had established that Illinois laws permitted only men to be admitted to the bar, and that the legislature had never intended to include women in this domain, he further added that members serving the bar must fulfill

> (28) such terms of admission *as would promote the proper administration of justice*. .

The phrase "the proper administration of justice" carries the implication that only male counsellors are capable of promoting and overseeing justice in the courts since males are the only ones who are said to have the "special qualifications" and the "skill and confidence" (*Bradwell* 1873) for legal office. The phrase "administration of justice" is used as something that can be read in this context to be a male province, and has been constructed in Text 1 as a privilege reserved for some, and delimited along sex lines.

The semantic re-alignment of terms can thus have far-reaching consequences for human individuals. The immense reach of the semantic redefinitions (whether in restricting or expanding linguistic scope) is unsurprising if one recognizes that the act of naming and defining the scope of the terms of discourse amounts to a claim to "semantic authority" (in the Bakhtinian sense) on the part of the speaker or writer who acts to control the discourse. Defining the terms of discourse not only isolates for the author and the directed audience what is to be meant by those terms, but delineating the meaning of these terms also constitutes a form of semantic positioning that goes into the making of a linguistic worldview (Bakhtin 1929: 152). Viewed in this way, the power of the determination of the meaning of linguistic terms may be better appreciated. For what can be more definitive and more discursively powerful than the authorial determination of what 'reality' should be taken as natural?

3.4 Choice of register and pragmatic power

The judicial opinion consistently employs one particular register which reinforces its formality, distance, and power. These aspects of pragmatic power are realized through various means. One of these is the use of standard language, which exclusively indexes the formal and educated setting of the law. The use of standard language is assumed to possess a "supposed logical superiority" (Kroch and Small 1978: 46), giving judicial discourse an aura of respectability and power. Setting aside the question of a standard accent (since I am dealing with written documents), the ultimate authority of these judicial texts is not just encased in the standard grammar of judicial rhetoric, it is also enshrined by its 'written-ness'. By this, I refer to the fact that judicial opinions are primarily written discourses. In the final analysis, it is the duty of faithful legal scribes to preserve these opinions in legal archives for the benefit of posterity. This process of enshrining the written opinions of the Courts in court reporters kept in law libraries (and even in this choice of locations, I note the exclusivity and general inaccessibility of law to the layperson) for future use is what makes this authority and power so enduring and accessible only to a privileged few.

Another means by which legal power is kept within the institution is the use of legal terminology throughout these texts, which marks out these texts as belonging to a specialized register and domain. Just as special terms of discourse define those who use them as members of the same group, the inaccessibility of these same terms to outsiders cut the latter group off as the Other. Legal terminology thus keeps members within the fold of the legal institution, and at the same time, they fence out those who do not belong to the institution. In this way, institutional identity is constructed through membership, and legal power is concentrated within its own camp, thus creating the distance between the lawgivers, interpreters and students of law and the lay population. The maintenance of boundaries, it is clear, is crucial in defining the separateness of law from that of the general public.

The gulf that separates the judicial community from the laypersons standing before the Court thus creates and supports an image of a detached authority that is inaccessible to the general public, but which still commands the public's attention. In all of these, the mystique of the Court is perpetuated and its power maintained. In short, the pragmatic power of the judiciary is constituted singly and collectively through the careful linguistic choices that are made in the production of judicial discourse and through the entire gamut of judicial roles, acts and activities that go to make up the judicial performance of speech acts. As Bourdieu has argued with respect to persons conferred with institutional power, "[i]t is through the effect of statutory assignation (*noblesse oblige*) that the ritual of institution produces its most 'real' effects: the person instituted feels obliged to comply with his definition, with the status of his function" (1991: 121). In this sense, the judge's power, as a realization of the Court's power, is a privilege that is his/hers to exercise, but the duty of the judge to act *qua* judge is dictated by the institutional norms of behaviour, which include dress codes and the use of the standard language.

3.5 Resources, choices, and ground rules: The process of discursive shifts

Sherzer (1990: 7) asserts that discourse is

> the locus of the expression of ideology and especially of the playing out and the working out of conflicts, tensions, and changes inherent in ideological systems. In focusing on the expression of ideology in discourse, it is important to pay attention to matters of detail, such as lists and orders within lists, which are most revealing of underlying beliefs.

However, I would further argue that an attempt at a linguistic indexing of ideology must at some point move away from the localized details of linguistic resources and the (ordering of) lists that Sherzer alludes to. As Sherzer has correctly maintained, discourse is the actualization and creation of grammar. But even given this important distinction between grammar and discourse, I think that consideration must be given to what is, relatively speaking at least, the more *global* level of discourse.

What follows is in three parts: first, the discursive shifts in the arguments are discussed as I view the texts, in chronological succession, as a continuing story about the life and the values of a culture as it undergoes social and political changes. In this respect, I focus on the specific arguments in each opinion and argue that the shifts in the discourses across time are facilitated by the specific changes made in the arguments in a specific socio-political context. Second, I discuss the differences in judicial styles that may be said to contribute to the shifts as they exert pressure on the nature of the judicial argumentation. Third, in the use of precedents, my argument is that specific choices made in this respect define the direction in which the opinion is constructed. As a particular universe of discourse is defined by the appeal to one precedent rather than another, the movements across texts are thus effected.

3.5.1 The arguments and their socio-political contexts

A close reading of the two judicial opinions reveals that each of them, unsurprisingly perhaps, revolves around one, or more, central argument(s). Here, I recall briefly the main arguments in each text. In Text 1, the argument that was used to deny Myra Bradwell of her right to be admitted to the Illinois bar is carried through by a series of images that feed into the doctrine of separate spheres. One of these is the masculinization of the law and the legal profession. By describing the legal profession as a masculine enterprise, Justice Bradley painted a picture of the bar as a totally unsuitable place for women. He writes:

> (29) But I am not prepared to say that it is one of her fundamental rights and privileges to be admitted into every office and position, including those which require highly special qualifications and demanding special responsibilities . . in my opinion, in view of the peculiar characteristics, destiny, and mission of woman, it is within the province of the legislature to ordain what offices, positions, and callings shall be filled and discharged by men, and shall receive the benefit of those energies and responsibilities, and that decision and firmness which are presumed to predominate in the sterner sex (Text 1).

In contrast to masculine "responsibilities" are feminine "destiny and mission". This characterization of feminine duties in terms of biological fate and determinism has the effect of fixing female identities and interests "before the law" (Schultz 1992: 299). If women's identities and natures are already predetermined by biology, Justice Bradley's attitude is a simple endorsement of that 'fact', a 'fact' that the Court claimed it was powerless to change.

Writing on behalf of a unanimous Court, Justice Brewer stated from the outset:

> (30) That woman's physical structure and the performance of maternal functions place her at a disadvantage in the struggle for subsistence is obvious (Text 2).

In this 'factual' pronouncement, the image of the physical weakness of woman and the naturalization of females in their roles as mothers are fixed as premises for the argument that disallows women to work for long hours outside the home. The restriction of work hours is cast in terms of the language of protection and care. By such a linguistic transformation of a potentially harmful social condition into a legal responsibility, which also appealed to the utilitarian principle "for the benefit of all" (Text 2), the Court justified the legislation based on an essentialism of gender differences. In both Texts 1 and 2, characteristics of gender exert a totalizing effect.

Each of these judicial texts may be seen first, as embodying a tale within itself and second, as exerting future effects, all from a single perspective. The function of judicial discourse is not simply a description of the social and legal relations between members in the community as told by the judicial speaker/writer, but is, more importantly, also the constitution of the community's present, future life and past history. Both Texts 1 and 2 inscribe within them the story of the life of an aspect of American society in the late 1800s. In this story, males and females exist on an unequal footing, each occupying a separate domain and each living out distinct social functions or roles. The role of the law, as is evident from these texts, is to reinforce, maintain, and perpetuate this complementarity of relations in the pre-established social equilibrium.

Since judges are members of both the legal, social, political and cultural institutions, the texts they produce and the terms of their discourses reflect not simply personal idiosyncracies and beliefs but also, more generally, the moods of the world which they inhabit. That Justice Bradley and Justice Brewer appear more conservative judges (by today's standard) is as much a personal statement about themselves as it is a pronouncement about the socio-cultural and political economy of their times. The separate sphere doctrine, for instance, is surely not a doctrine which either Justices Bradley or Brewer single-handedly created *ex nihilo*. Rather, it is a historical legacy originating from the days of William Blackstone in nineteenth-century England, thus attesting to the influence and reach of English Common Law. The influence of history and the pressures exerted by the ruling social order as well as existing laws are all crucial contexts which must be borne in mind when considering how and why particular judicial opinions are formulated in the manner that they are. Similarly, the social and political changes that accompany each succession of governmental administration, which in turn restore judges of particular political leanings in the courts are the factors that brought about the changes in the law as reflected in the writings and rulings of judges. As we shall see, it is no accident that Chief Justice Burger and Justice Blackmun constitute a different type of voice in the Courts than the justices of earlier times, for they are the products of a different era. However, this is not to say that judges are totally bound by these socio-cultural and political forces.

Whether a judge chooses to affirm public sentiments or to strike out against dissenting voices, these are indeed choices that a judge can make, and has made, even if there are limits imposed on their creativity.

3.5.2 Judicial styles

In their study of small-claims courts, Conley and O'Barr (1990) established that the personality and the individual style of the judge may bias the decision in particular directions (1990: 82). Judges are said to range on a continuum of styles, with the rule-oriented ones on one end, and the relational judges on the other. Rule-oriented judges are strict adherents to the principles of law; their role is to enforce these legal principles. Such judges tend to emphasize the 'objective' and unchanging nature of the law, and they are often reluctant to recognize exceptions. The relational judges, in contrast, are characterized by their treatment of law, not overtly as unchanging principles, but as a means to promote and effect more harmonious relationships between feuding parties. The law and the judge, in this light, thus serve as mediators. While the rule-oriented judge overplays the law's authority, the relational judge projects law as a compromise. These two styles represent two opposite extremes on a continuum of styles, for there are judges who display both rule-oriented and relational tendencies in different settings. These categories are merely convenient points of reference and are not static positions that individual judges unchangingly occupy.

Judicial styles have been viewed in terms of six modalities of argumentation (Bobbitt 1982, 1991):

- historical (emphasizing the original intent of the Framers of the Constitution)
- textual (stressing the ongoing social contract and contemporary meanings and use of the words of provisions)
- doctrinal (which relies on precedents or commentaries of precedents)
- structural (stressing the results of the structures of government and the relationship between the government and the people as created by the Constitution)
- prudential (in which political and economic circumstances determine a decision)
- ethical (which emphasizes the ethos of American institutions and the American people).

Bobbitt noted "what is usually called the *style* of a particular judge, as well as the very different notions of style in particular eras, can be explained as a preference for one type of argument over others" (1982: 8). Bobbitt added further that one often finds within a judicial opinion a combination of modalities rather than a single mode of argumentation working in isolation. By employing Bobbitt's modalities, therefore, the link may be made between judicial styles and the form of judicial arguments.

It is to be noted that *Bradwell* and *Muller* make constant appeals to rules of law (hence qualifying these judicial authors as tending towards the rule-oriented end), the difference being which particular rules are appealed to, and to what purpose these appeals to rules of law are put. Such a characterization is, however, plainly unhelpful as it glosses over the subtle similarities and differences that are exhibited in these texts. I believe Bobbitt's six modalities provide a more fruitful interpretation of these texts in terms of the judicial styles that define them.

Justice Bradley in *Bradwell* employed a combination of styles:

> Being contrary to the rules of the common law and the usages of Westminster Hall from time immemorial, it could not be supposed that the legislature had intended to adopt any different rule. . The claim that, under the fourteenth amendment of the Constitution, which declares that no State shall make or enforce any law which shall abridge the privileges and immunities of citizens of the United States, the statute law of Illinois, or the common law prevailing in that State, can no longer be set up as a barrier against the right of females to pursue any lawful employment for a livelihood (. .), assumes that it is one of the privileges and immunities of women as citizens to engage in any and every profession, occupation, or employment in civil life. . The constitution of the family organization, which is founded in the divine ordinance, as well as in the nature of things, indicated the domestic sphere as that which properly belongs to the domain and functions of womanhood (Text 1).

The above selection of some crucial portions of the argument in Text 1 shows that the judicial author employs a combination of the historical (appealing to the intent of the legislature and the common law), the structural (specifying what State and citizen can or cannot do), and the ethical (stressing the natural order and invoking the American family as a treasured institution) modes to legitimate his opinion. The emphasis that Justice Bradley placed on original intent and American family values lays down the ground work for a conservative decision that upholds the social ideology that woman's place is in the home. In contrast, Justice Brewer in *Muller* made primary use of the textual mode of argumentation:

> As minors, though not to the same extent, she has been looked upon in the courts as needing especial care that her rights may be preserved. Education was long denied her, and while now the doors of the school room are opened and her opportunities for acquiring knowledge are great, yet even with that and the consequent increase of capacity for business affairs it is still true that in the struggle for subsistence she is not an equal competitor with her brother. Though limitations upon personal and contractual rights may be removed by legislation, there is that in her disposition and habits of life which will operate against a full assertion of those rights. She will still be where some legislation to protect her seems necessary to secure a real equality of rights (Text 2).

Text 2 thus argued from the viewpoint of a continued need to treat women as a special class in need of protection, hence legitimating the judicial move to maintain the status quo.

Not only do these particular forms of judicial argumentation characterize the opinion as a judicial opinion, they also reflect the preferred style of the judicial writer, thus determining the distinct character of each opinion. These modalities (i.e., the modes in which judges make arguments in the judicial setting), as a reflection of judicial style and personality, thus exert a fair amount of influence on the shape in which the opinion takes. The shifts in the discourse are thus effected by the particular choices made in the style of argumentation employed. Apart from arguments and styles, another factor that affects the direction of discourse is the appeal to specific precedents.

3.5.3 The use of precedents

It has been said that "the essence of a legal system such as ours . . is its reliance on precedent as a determinant of decisions" (Abraham 1981:771). The appeal to precedents is thus an established legal practice whose importance lies in the fact that precedents not only establish points of law that have been previously debated, but also serve to lend support to court rulings. The Court's appeal to precedents, therefore, functions as a means by which the Court could reassert and reaffirm its authority, while at the same time enabling the Court to maintain its image of rationality – that it anchors its reasoning not on capricious moods but on an established line of decisions. In other words, the appeal to precedents makes the court's decision appear less arbitrary or whimsical. In addition, by appealing to precedents, the court also reconnects itself with the past, thus maintaining the continuity of tradition and history that is so important to the law's preservation of its own validity. Precedents are, as White says, "a kind of bridge from one world to the other" (1988:406). But what is even more important in this connection with the past is the manner in which the past is interpreted. Abraham (1981:772) characterizes this process of interpretation as follows:

> By anchoring the justification for both easy and hard decisions in a past – in history and tradition – a legal system circumscribes the authority of its judges, who must make decisions in the present. The process of interpreting the past thereby becomes one of the defining features of legal reasoning. Furthermore, in our system it is not the past itself but the method used to interpret the past which binds decisions in the present. It is through interpretation that the past is constituted and reconstituted in the present.

Precedents are, however, not always cited only to affirm a particular decision. There are, in fact, a variety of reasons for citing particular precedents. For example, a case may be cited to show that the reasoning used in the two cases under comparison are not in agreement. Hence, interesting observations may be made with regard to (1) what precedents are actually cited in the judicial text studied and the reason(s) for the citation, and (2) under what circumstances has the case under consideration been cited by other judicial texts, i.e. served as a precedent for other cases. Observing the use made of specific precedents in a judicial text is thus expected to yield interesting insights into why certain choices are made by the judicial author, and how a particular universe of discourse is defined.

No precedent is cited in Text 1, and this is itself a revealing factor. Justice Bradley was also a member of the Court presiding over the famous *Slaughterhouse Cases,*[12] where in his dissent, he opposed the Court's decision, which ruled against a group of (male) butchers who argued that their right to an occupation was threatened by the state monopoly. In his dissent, Justice Bradley wrote (*Slaughterhouse Cases* (1872):112, 113, 119):

> Is it one of the rights and privileges of a citizen of the United States to pursue such civil employment as he may choose to adopt, subject to such reasonable regulations as may be prescribed by law? . . in my judgment, the right of any citizen to follow whatever lawful employment he chooses to adopt (submitting himself to all lawful regulations) is one of his most valuable rights, and one which the legislature of a State cannot invade, whether restrained by its own constitution or not. . Inhabitants. .as citizens of the United States, lay claim to every one of the privileges and immunities which have been enumerated; and among these none is more essential and fundamental than the right to follow such profession or

> employment as each one may choose, subject only to uniform regulations equally applicable to all.

The decision for the *Slaughterhouse Cases* came just a day before the ruling on *Bradwell,* and Justice Bradley in effect ignored (through his silence) his own precedent by ruling against Myra Bradwell's right to pursue an occupation of her own choice. Apparently, "the right of any citizen to follow whatever lawful employment he chooses to adopt" did not somehow also extend to Myra Bradwell which, he argued, applied to the butchers in Louisiana. It is in itself an interesting point that Justice Bradley saw the two cases as different, though the two cases seem to involve a similar legal principle – an inalienable right of citizenship to pursue a livelihood. What was the most valuable of rights in one case became subjected to "reasonable regulations as may be prescribed by law" in another. By framing the two cases within different sets of discourses, Justice Bradley gave us an insight into his ideology regarding his (unequal) treatment for the sexes.

A check with *Shepard's US Citations* shows that *Bradwell* has been cited over two hundred times (1994: 1.1: 1070). The only time that the *Bradwell* decision has been overtly criticized is in the case of *Frontiero v. Richardson* (1973).[13] In a plurality opinion, Justice Brennan, citing *Bradwell,* among other cases, ruled that (*Frontiero v. Richardson,* (1973): 684, 686)

> [t]here can be no doubt that our Nation has had a long and unfortunate history of sex discrimination. Traditionally, such discrimination was rationalized by an attitude of "romantic paternalism" which, in practical effect, put women, not on a pedestal, but in a cage. . Moreover, since sex, like race and national origin, is an immutable characteristic determined solely by the accident of birth, the imposition of special disabilities upon the members of a particular sex because of their sex would seem to violate "the basic concept of our system that legal burdens should bear some relationship to individual responsibility. ." *Weber v. Aetna Casualty and Surety Co. 406 U.S. 164 (1972).*

Bradwell's arguments, based on female fragility and special protection for women are therefore criticized and dismissed a century later as a case of 'romantic paternalism'. In this citation, the role of the appeal to a precedent is not to affirm a past decision but to disagree with its principles.

On another occasion, the *Bradwell* ruling is challenged over its continued validity and relevance in more modern times. Chief Judge Coffin's opinion in *Women's Liberation Union of Rhode Island v. Israel* (1975)[14] stated that (pp.108–109):

> Appellants suggest that the purpose of 3–8–5 is to protect women because "bars are rough places." They offer no evidence whatever to establish that violence is specially prevalent in bars with class C licenses (. .); or that women, more than men, need protection when violence erupts in their presence; or that prohibiting the service of beverages to women, while allowing their presence, preserves them from harm. Appellants place their major reliance on stare decisis, i.e., on cases in which the Court did indeed content itself with stereotypes. . But the authority of those precedents, as the district court amply demonstrated in its comprehensive opinions, has waned with the metamorphosis of the attitudes which fed them. What then was gallantry now appears Victorian condescension or even misogyny, and this cultural evolution is now reflected in the Constitution.

In these two instances, *Bradwell* was challenged on its (continued) soundness. Thus, one set of arguments is displaced and replaced by another set of reasoning, hence effecting the discursive shift that is evident from one text to another, and from one period to another.

One of the cases cited in Text 2 is *Lochner v. New York* (1905).[15] The *Muller* Court chose to distinguish *Muller* from *Lochner,* by arguing that due to the difference in physical structure between the sexes, "legislation designed for [a woman's] protection may be sustained, even when like legislation is not necessary for men and could not be sustained" (Text 2), the lack of restrictions on the male being amply illustrated in the *Lochner* decision. *Lochner*, then, served as a contrast in the Court's explicit and differential treatment of the sexes. An additional point of interest in the *Muller* opinion is that the Court chose not only to recall various precedents that involved the qualified power to contract for all individuals in all circumstances, but also to appeal to public opinion as an influencing factor, thus setting itself up as a precedent in this respect. In Justice Brewer's words (*Muller*, pp.420–421):

> The legislation and opinions. .are significant of a widespread belief that woman's physical structure and the functions she performs in consequence thereof, justify special legislation restricting or qualifying the conditions under which she should be permitted to toil. Constitutional questions, it is true, are not settled by even a consensus of present public opinion, for it is the peculiar value of a written constitution that it places in unchanging form limitations upon legislative action, and thus gives a permanence and stability to popular government which otherwise would be lacking. At the same time, when a question of fact is debated and debatable, and the extent to which a special constitutional limitation goes is affected by the truth in respect to that fact, a widespread and long continued belief concerning it is worthy of consideration. We take judicial cognizance of all matters of general knowledge.

Hence, both precedents and, at times, public opinion are given "judicial cognizance," thus influencing the nature of particular judicial decisions.

Muller, according to *Shepard's Citations* (1994: 1.3: 301–302), has been cited over four hundred times, this being a comment on both the enthusiastic support and the equally overwhelming disapproval over the opinion at different points in times by different courts. Here, I discuss two such citations. The first of these is the case of *Radice v. New York* (1924),[16] where Justice Sutherland, writing on behalf of the Court, upholds a New York statute which, like the Oregon one in *Muller*, restricted the working hours for women. In an opinion that cited the language of *Muller* as both "applicable and controlling" and using language that is almost identical to *Muller*, Justice Sutherland says:

> The answer of the State is that night work of the kind prohibited, so injuriously affects the physical condition of women, and so threatens to impair their peculiar and natural functions, and so exposes them to the dangers and menaces incident to night life in large cities, that a statute prohibiting such work falls within the police power of the State to preserve and promote the public health and welfare. . We cannot say that the conclusion is without warrant. The loss of restful night's sleep can not be fully made up by sleep in the day time, especially in busy cities, subject to the disturbances incident to modern life. The injurious consequences were thought by the legislature to bear more heavily against women than men, and, considering their more delicate organism, there would seem to be good reason for so thinking. . The language used by this Court in *Muller*. .in respect of the physical limitations of women, is applicable and controlling …

This affirmation of *Muller* is, however, not present in *Poe v. Werner* (1974).[17] Fifty years later, writing on the legitimacy of the regulations on hair length for male prison inmates, Chief District Judge Sheridan reduced *Muller* to a footnote (*Poe v. Werner* (1974): 1019, Fn.6):

> In *Muller v. Oregon*. ., the Court established that women could constitutionally be treated differently from men. . . [This case epitomizes] the traditional rational basis test in equal protection analysis. While the Court has never explicitly overruled *Muller*, . .it appears that the rationale of [this case] has been undermined by *Reed*, *Frontiero*, *Kahn* and *Geduldig* in which the Court scrutinized more closely the relationship between the sex classification and the purpose of the legislative enactment of which it was a part.

Thus, Judge Sheridan dismissed *Muller* as no longer having any precedential value, adopting instead a stricter test to assess the appropriateness of legislative actions.

The story within each of these judicial texts therefore goes beyond the boundaries of the text itself. Each text recalls a history of what had been, through its constant references to established statutes and its appeal to the social order. A crucial point that has been noted in legal scholarship and judicial criticism is that the act of invoking particular precedents actively influences the Court's decision in some particular direction, since the calling up of one precedent rather than another carries with it the judge's choice to establish or to negate a particular universe of discourse in which his or her opinion will be cast. In short, a particular judicial text not only serves to establish and to maintain existing social relations, but it also plays a central role in maintaining historical continuity with the past by its inter-textual associations with other texts. This continuity, which stretches back into a past that can be as remote as the judge chooses through the exercised choice of precedents, also reaches into the future by the text's establishment of itself as a precedent for future actions. Hence, the story that is told by the text is one that is rich in past history, relevant to the present condition, and loaded with future possibilities.

The harmony (when courts agree) and conflicts (when dissents are made known) between voices in the judicial discourse thus serve as barometers, recording the different moods of the judicial community. The maintenance of order, the struggle for ideological dominance, and the negotiation of human relations all employ the text as an arena where verbal duels are constantly staged. But if the text is the medium for voices in battle, then discourse is the terrain on which these battles are fought. The determination of which set of relations should dominate or which will in turn define the new terms of 'reality' is discursively effected as new terms are forged and old terms are either redefined or replaced. Such new definitions of new world orders through the discursive process of the establishment of a dominant voice result in the formation of new knowledge and power relations, in the Foucauldian sense. Such new knowledge and power relations in turn are the contending determinants of newer and ever-emerging terms of negotiation, as is evident if Text 1 is contrasted with more recent texts, where the terms defining a more equal footing between the sexes have replaced the terms of destiny and biology. Discursive shifts result when the replacement of old terms by new ones is completed.

The freedom and the power of judges to create and innovate new arguments are however not absolute. Even in the freedom of choice to create a text that is consistent with his/her own ideology, the judge is nevertheless a situated being, deeply embedded in the nexus of socio-cultural obligations by virtue of his/her membership in the society and culture. As White (1985:239) has said, granted that the law (and its legal officers) can be immensely powerful, this power is nevertheless kept in check by (1) the separation of powers and (2) the obligation to explain in a way that is justifiable. The law and its agents are therefore required to recognize other forms of power, such as public opinion and social ideology, and also that legal officers are required to justify their actions not only to colleagues in the field, but also to their own institution and to society at large. These are the constraints, among many others, inherent in any socio-political economy that the judge is bound by. Seen in this way, it is easy to recognize that even the most powerful of judges is not an absolutely free agent, accountable to no one.

The above discussion of arguments, styles, and precedents hopes to have shown that it is under such conditions of freedom and constraints that judges exercise their choices in making their rulings, and in the production as well as the interpretation of texts. The different factors that influence the judicial decision-making process are viewed here as individual, socio-cultural, and institutional resources that can be realized within defined boundaries, boundaries which change with time and which are modified and redefined from judge to judge and as one era succeeds another. These resources may be said to comprise a semiotic web, because they interrelate and penetrate one another with no clear-cut boundaries; each resource is a potential realization of meanings and implications that can only be interpreted and valued within its own context of operation. The judicial decision-making process is thus conceived of as a journey through a garden path of choices, with each one taken up or abandoned in favour of some other choices as and when the individual deems appropriate. In all these realizations of choice paths, shifts in the discourse are brought about as new choices are privileged over old ones. In short, the simultaneous convergence of choices made by the judicial author has profound effects on the nature of judicial opinions, as an examination of the two opinions considered here have indicated.

4. Summary

My analysis has concentrated on the terms that index gender, gender roles, and power, and found that how each of these terms are used has profound effects on the outcome of each opinion. The grammatical analysis of subject-verb predication, mood, and modality showed that power is differentially distributed in the judicial context. The Court defines the issues to be discussed, the manner in which they are discussed, and their outcome. The Court's authority is conveyed, maintained, and constantly reaffirmed through its use of performative-style verbs, reinforced by modals expressing moral and legal obligations, and carried through the declarative mood. The indexing of gender and power is also found to involve a semantic restriction of the scope of application of terms, such as what constitutes personhood and rights. The power of the judiciary as reflected in the discourse is further explored in terms of an examination of the choice of the standard language. In this respect, I argued that the choice of the standard language further enhances the authority of the Court especially when this choice is consonant with the widely accepted standard-language ideology that equates authority and power with the knowledge and use of the standard language. Finally, I looked at how each text is shaped by the textual choices made from available resources in each context, and how different forces (such as personal style, judicial conventions, types of precedents, and socio-political pressures) operating together on the judicial author jointly act in the creation of the judicial opinion. The particular manners of indexing, either through lexical, grammatical or semantic means, have the effect of defining the universe of discourse (and its scope) from which certain judicial arguments operated. The linguistic indexing and inscription of social categories like gender roles and domains of power not only fixes the universe of discourse but also reflect the nature of competing ideologies operating simultaneously within any given context.

Chapter 4

Women are persons after all

The rights of Sally Reed and Jane Roe

> To most women, the law is a foreign country with an unintelligible tongue, alien mores, secret traps, uncontrollable and unresponsive dynamics, obscure but rigid dogmas, barbaric and draconian rituals, and consequences as scary as they are incomprehensible. Actually, this is true for most men as well. The difference is that those who can and do make law work for them, those who designed it so it would work for them, as if they were the whole world, are men – specifically, white upper-class men. Women reflect this reality in their view, that if you try to use the law, it is likely to blow up in your face as to help. Law is Kafka's trial, Dickens's Bleak House. Mostly women feel that the law is not about them, has no idea who they are or what they face or how they think or feel, has nothing to say to them and can do nothing for them. When the law and their life collide, it is their life that gets the worst of it.
>
> – Catharine MacKinnon (1993: 109–110)

1. Preliminaries

The two judicial texts to be examined here are taken from two more recent cases: *Reed v. Reed* (1971) and *Roe v. Wade* (1973). As in the previous chapter, I will begin with some background information for these two cases, and then proceed with an analysis of each of the opinions resulting from these cases. This chapter attempts to establish the point that the judicial rhetoric has indeed changed and details how it has changed since the days of Myra Bradwell and Mrs Elmer Gotcher. However, I will also argue that though the changes are noticeable, they are not significant in that they do not guarantee for women the full rights of personhood that they deserve.

2. Background

2.1 Suspect classifications: Sally Reed fights back (1971)

Since the days of overt gender discrimination suffered by women like Myra Bradwell and Mrs Elmer Gotcher, the tide turned in favour of women and minorities between the years 1963 and 1972 (Lindgren and Taub 1988:37). The Equal Pay Act (1963) and Title VII of the Civil Rights Act (1964) were both enacted in Congress. In addition, Title IX of the Educational Amendments Act (1972) prohibited discrimination in providing educational opportunities on the basis of sex. In the state courts, the place of gender in the law finally gained attention in the final years of the 1960s. It was under these sweeping changes in the political, legal and social arenas that the case of *Reed v. Reed* (1971) came before the United States Supreme Court.

Reed v. Reed has been described as a turning point in women's battle for gender justice in the courts. Wexler (2001:39) noted the significance of *Reed* as follows:

> When the Supreme Court handed down its opinion in *Reed v. Reed* in November of 1971, the decision made headlines across the country. For the first time since the Fourteenth Amendment had gone into effect in 1868, the Court had struck down a state law on the ground that it discriminated against women in violation of the Equal Protection Clause.

Richard Lynn Reed died intestate (i.e. without leaving a will) in Ada County, Idaho, in 1967. His adoptive parents, Sally and Cecil Reed, were separated before Richard's death. About seven months after Richard died, Sally Reed sought to be the administratrix of her son's estate. Cecil Reed, the adoptive father of the deceased, filed a competing petition in the Idaho Probate Court, seeking to have him, Cecil, appointed the administrator. After a joint hearing in the Probate Court, the court ruled in favour of Cecil Reed, in accordance with an Idaho code that gave preference to Cecil Reed because as the code then specifies, "[o]f several persons claiming and equally entitled to administer, males must be preferred to females".

After her first appeal against this decision was not acted on, Sally Reed subsequently brought a suit before the U.S. Supreme Court to contest the constitutionality of the Idaho statute. A unanimous Supreme Court struck down and dismissed the Idaho statute as unconstitutional, citing the principle of equal protection for all under the laws. *Reed* is considered by some legal scholars as an important one because it establishes a new trend of stricter constitutional scrutiny in the courts, making gender a suspect classification. What is also significant about *Reed* is that for the first time, the Equal Protection Clause was successfully applied in a constitutional challenge; thus, *Reed* has the effect of implicitly overturning all gender-based discrimination cases prior to it. *Reed v. Reed,* therefore, may be said to usher in "the beginning of a new judicial era" (Lindgren and Taub 1988: 47) which sees the Court taking a more serious look at cases involving gender discrimination.

2.2 The right of choice: Jane Roe and reproductive freedom (1973)

According to Justice Ruth Bader Ginsburg, *Roe v.* Wade "became and remains a storm center" because "the Court ventured too far in the change it ordered and presented an incomplete justification for its action" (1995: 282). This "storm center" has its beginnings in a small Dallas town in 1969, when Norma McCorvey found herself pregnant for the third time. Having no resources to support herself, she sought to have an abortion. However, Norma soon learnt that an abortion was then illegal in Texas under an 1854 Texas statute, and in her despair, she looked into the possibilities of having an illegal abortion.

Two lawyers, Sarah Weddington and Linda Coffee, were at that time looking for a pregnant plaintiff to help them in their cause to challenge the Texas anti-abortion statute. Their search finally brought them to Dallas, and after a meeting with Norma, they decided that she would be their plaintiff to challenge the Texas law. The case of Jane Roe, as she came to be called to protect her identity at that time, later evolved into a class-action lawsuit that was argued twice: first in front of seven Supreme Court justices, and once again before the full nine-member Court. In a vote of 7-to-2, the case of *Roe v. Wade* (1973) was decided in favour of a woman's right to her own decision with regard to reproductive freedom. Text 4 in the Appendix is the majority opinion delivered by Justice Harry Blackmun.

Though *Roe* may not be a straightforward case involving gender-based discrimination, it is nevertheless a case where gender issues are implicated. One of the many controversial issues in *Roe* has to do with who is entitled to make decisions about female reproductive choices. The debates in *Roe*, and the debates that have been generated by it, oscillate constantly between the extent of governmental intervention permissible in what is fundamentally, as the Court established in 1973, a personal decision on the one hand, and the infringement upon individual rights on the other. The case also raises the issue of the competing rights of the mother, the foetus, and the father. But underlying all these debates is one central issue that makes *Roe* a case about gender: Who has control over the female? Justice Ginsburg, however, wrote that *Roe* involves a broader issue, which she describes as follows (1995:289):

> I appreciate the intense divisions of opinion on the moral question and recognize that abortion today cannot fairly be described as nothing more than birth control delayed. The conflict, however, is not simply one between a fetus' interests and a woman's interests, narrowly conceived, nor is the overriding issue state versus private control of a woman's body for a span of nine months. Also in the balance is a woman's autonomous charge of her full life's course … her ability to stand in relation to man, society, and the state as an independent, self-sustaining, equal citizen.

This question of control over the female and her full status as "an independent, self-sustaining equal citizen" with rights equal to any man is a question that has long been an issue in American law. Case after case can be cited (*Bradwell* and *Muller* being just two examples) from the nineteenth century through the greater part of the twentieth century to show that every form of restriction over female participation in public life has something to do with how much right a woman should be accorded so as to ensure that traditional male control over the female is not eroded.[1] Far from being a case that is unlike the other three cases discussed here, *Roe* addresses questions that are on the one hand not entirely new and, on the other continue to be of contemporary relevance, as the unrelenting debates in abortion rights show.

Roe also addresses the issue of personhood, which is also a key issue in *Bradwell*, and in many other cases. *Roe* thus provides an opportunity to discuss how this issue – what constitutes personhood in the eyes of the law with regard to gender – has evolved and changed through the course of a century.

In addition to the above, *Roe* also provides an opportunity to discuss the issues of rhetorical challenges, discursive shifts and the process of negotiations of rights as well as the struggles for control at the site of an ongoing living discourse. By looking at *Roe* and the other judicial texts studied here, I hope to formulate an analysis that will contribute, from a linguist's viewpoint, to current debates on the abortion issue in particular, and on the nature of gender justice.

3. An analysis of *Reed* and *Roe*

3.1 Lexical choices

In terms of gender roles, the language used in Text 3 indexes the male as "spouse", "son", "father", "brother", and "male relative". These terms comprise a listing of how the male can stand in relation to the female under the Idaho Code that was then being questioned by the Court:

> (1) Indeed, under 15–312, a woman whose *spouse* dies intestate has a preference over a *son, father, brother, or any other male relative* of the decedent. (Text 3)

The Court's challenge to Section 15–314 of the Idaho code in *Reed* makes it clear however, that the Court does not endorse the statute's preferential treatment given to the male parent over the female parent. Text 4, in contrast, shows the male simply indexed in his situated legal stance as "appellee":

> (2) *The appellee* and certain amici argue that the fetus is a "person" within the language and meaning of the Fourteenth Amendment. (Text 4)

On the whole, both Text 3 and Text 4 exhibit an absence of lexical terms such as those found in the earlier texts that display the tendency to essentialize male social roles and attributes. The overt absence of such sexism provides the first hint of the difference and the shift in the judicial attitudes and ideology towards gender and gender roles in the Supreme Court.

An additional point of interest that pertains to Text 4 concerns the use of the word "burden" to describe the onus on the (male) appellee's part to prove to the Court that the State's interest in imposing limits on a woman's right to choose is justified and legitimate. In other words, the onus rests on the appellee (who represents the State of Texas) to convince the Court of the rationale and legitimacy of the State's interest in the case. Though "burden" is used in a technical way in the legal context, it is still significant that the indexing of the State's duty as a "burden" stands in stark contrast to the tone set in earlier cases where the (female) plaintiff is usually allocated with the burden of proof of her legitimacy. For instance, that Myra Bradwell had to file a lawsuit to establish her right to practise law may be said to be an imposed burden on her to show the Court that her right to an occupation is one that is sacred and guaranteed by law. Similarly, the fact that Mrs Gotcher in *Muller* had to seek the Court's judgement on the question of a woman's right to contract in the public sphere is evidence that it is a woman's duty to establish that she has the same right to operate publicly, unhindered by restrictive laws.

Unlike Text 1, which refers to the female as "the plaintiff", Text 3 uses the direct indexical "Sally Reed". In this same regard, Text 4 contains the uncontroversial index "woman". No attempt may be discerned from Texts 3 and 4 to dehumanize or to belittle the individuality of the female.

Text 3 has little to yield in terms of indirect indexical relations pertaining to the female, since all that is relevant in the context of Text 3 is the role of an administrator (of an estate). This is itself a statement of change in the Court's argumentation since the absence of any kind of suggestive characterization of the male or the female, other than what is relevant to the issue at hand, tells us how far the Court has come in terms of what it sees and defines as *the* important issue – namely, the question of the equal standing of male and female persons with regard to estate administration. Thus, in my opinion, the Court is at this point in time much more focused on addressing the relevant points of law than in endorsing conventional ideas of the 'proper' roles of men and women in American society, witnessed in earlier cases like *Bradwell* and *Muller*.

However, Text 4 provides an interesting contrast to the two earlier texts as it paints a totally different picture of the female. Gone are her dependencies on the male sex and her in-born biological weaknesses ascribed to her in earlier judicial discourses. Text 4, for example, does not indicate or dictate what a woman's attributes are or what her roles ought to be. Instead, the opinion speaks in terms of the woman's right to choose and of her privacy with regard to her decision and determination to exercise her rights in the abortion decision. Though the female's role as a *potential* mother is recognized in the text, motherhood is not essentialized as a necessary part of the woman's role in life. The Court thus refrains from saying what female (and male) roles or the feminine (and masculine) attributes are supposed to be, which is a prevalent feature in the earlier texts.

The above analysis of the relative absence of terms indexing both the male and the female, their social roles, activities, and attributes in an essentialist manner attests to the visible changes in more recent judicial rhetoric on gender relations and the social and legal construction of male and female roles. This difference is hardly surprising: the American society of earlier years is a different one from that of more recent times. It would have been surprising if there had *not* been any change at all. However, the point remains that judicial attitudes and ideology have moved with the times (though not always at the desired rate). As a more enlightened Court moved towards a more contemporary outlook on gender issues, the more contemporary character of judicial discourse reflects such a change in the Court's attitude by registering a general absence of blatant essentialization of gender roles. Where the Court once spoke of the rightful positions of men and women in the social context, it now speaks in terms of rights entitlements and equal protection of the law. The change in the terms of judicial discourse must thus by duly noted.

3.2 Grammatical patterning

3.2.1 Subject-verb predication

Unlike Texts 1 and 2, Texts 3 and 4 appeal to slightly different sources of authority.

Recall that in Texts 1 and 2, divine ordinance, history, religion, and nature are featured in arguments that naturalize the role of men as protectors and providers and women as mothers and wives, thus successfully excluding female participation. As can be seen from Table 5, Texts 3 and 4 made appeals to rights, legal principles, and linguistic meanings, thus underscoring the linguistic nature of law. For example, note the situated appeal to "the meaning of the Fourteenth Amendment":

> (3) On the other hand, the appellee conceded on rearguments that no case could be cited that holds that a fetus is a person *within the meaning of the Fourteenth Amendment.* (Text 4)

The shift from a rhetoric that once privileged a discourse that essentializes women's and men's roles to one that foregrounds the legal entitlements of individuals and the real meaning of equal protection signals a change in socio-cultural appreciations of gender roles and also a judicial enlightenment of views that is crucial to the battle for equality between the sexes in law and in society.

Judicial power is also manifested in the grammatical subject-verb collocation in these two texts; see Table 6. Though the legal authorities are most concerned with justifying and grounding their arguments in facts and in reason, the Court, for one, can also "judicially notice", which means that the Court can simply state and take a point of law for granted (because it has already been previously established) without having to provide further proofs of legitimacy. Furthermore, what a law or court can establish, another law or court can strike down, rendering the targeted law invalid, unconstitutional, or

Table 5. Sources of authority

Authority	Text 3	Text 4
LAW	this Court	The Constitution
	we	the Court
	Section 15–314 of the Idaho Code	individual justices
	the Fourteenth Amendment's command	First, Fourth, Fifth, Ninth, Fourteenth Amendments
	the equal protection of the laws	the Bill of Rights
	15–312	the District Court
	statute	we
	the object of the legislation	the Texas statute
	the Idaho Supreme Court	the judiciary
GOVERNMENT	State	the State
	Idaho	state regulation
	state object	Texas
REASON	rational relationship	compelling state interests
		basis
		reason
RIGHTS	–	right of personal privacy
		rights to the people
		fundamental rights
		choice
LANGUAGE/ CONCEPTS	–	the concept of liberty
		the meaning of the Fourteenth Amendment
		the word "person"
Precedents	–	a line of decisions
		Union Pacific R.Co. v. Botsford (1891)
		Eisenstadt
		Griswold
		Stanley
		Loving
		Skinner
		Pierce
		Meyer
Other disciplines	–	Medicine
		Philosophy
		Theology
		The development of man's knowledge
		Present medical knowledge

Table 6. Some examples of grammatical subjects and verbs indexing power

Text	Subject	Verb
3	(by) this Court	review
	we	noted/examined/considered/ concluded/judicially notice/hold/reversed
	Idaho [i.e. the statute]	established/den[ies]
	The Equal Protection Clause of that amendment	does deny/forbids
	The Idaho Supreme Court	concluded
4	The Court/individual justices/we	has recognized/found/agree/ held
	The District Court	determined
	The State	impose/deny/decide/may regulate
	The Constitution	does not define
	Texas	may override

unacceptable. These are the extents of the powers of the Court in particular, and are true of the other sources of authority in general. The use of verbs of saying in most instances as in Table 6 above is a good illustration of how awesome judicial power is as it literally enforces the Court's validity and authority through the linguistic act of verbal pronouncement. A case is said to be "noted" by the justices, which means the standing of the parties in the case is recognized by the Court as valid. Without such a judicial recognition, Sally Reed's appeal would have been summarily dismissed and there would her story end. In a similar manner, the Equal Protection Clause is said to forbid any "arbitrary legislative choice" that is made without sound justification:

> (4) To give a mandatory preference to members of either sex over members of the other, merely to accomplish the elimination of hearings on the merits, is to make the very kind of arbitrary legislative choice *forbid*den by *the Equal Protection Clause of the Fourteenth Amendment*.... (Text 3)

In contrast to the above grammatical patterning, which indexes the power of the judiciary, the lack of power on the part of other parties is indexed in the following use of verbs that signal little or no power:

Table 7. Some examples of grammatical subjects and verbs indexing powerless referents

Text	Subject	Verb
3	Sally Reed	appealed
	Widows	administer
	Male and female members	file
	persons/men and women	are
4	The appellee/appellant	failed/conceded
	She	is/chooses/carries

A number of observations can be made here. First, as has been previously noted, there is little power in acts of appeal and concessions compared to the power that is manifested in the use of verbs like "deny" and "order". The imbalance in the distribution of power in the legal context is clear. Second, the sparseness of examples in Table 7 above that I could draw from the two texts is indicative of the fact that in these texts (especially Text 4), the powerless agents are often not named as subjects, but as objects being acted upon. For example, "the woman" in (5) below is cast as a passive recipient of "a distressed life" rather than as someone in control of her life:

> (5) Maternity, or additional offspring, may force upon the woman a distressful life and future. (Text 4)

Third, in several cases throughout the texts, the powerless participants are not mentioned directly. Instead, their physical, emotional or mental states are often what get emphasized. For example, instead of "the woman", the example below shows that it is the woman's health that is highlighted in the judicial discussion:

> (6) Mental and physical health may be taxed by child care. (Text 4)

In other words, the powerlessness of these participants are reduced further as their welfare and interests, not their identities, are matters of judicial concern. In this way, their subjectivity is displaced in the texts.

3.2.2 Mood choice

The following are examples drawn from Texts 3 and 4 to illustrate the mood structure of these two texts:

(7) *We hold* that it does not. (Text 3)

(8) By providing dissimilar treatment for men and women who are thus similarly situated, *the challenged section violates* the Equal Protection Clause. . (Text 3)

(9) *The Constitution does* not define "person". .in so many words. (Text 4)

(10) *These interests are* separate and distinct. (Text 4)

As in the previous two texts, the use of the declarative mood in Texts 3 and 4 reinforces the power of the judges and the Court, a power that is accustomed to issuing statements of 'facts', and declaring the rule of law, in a manner that does not permit direct challenge to its authoritative stance. We note in the above examples that when the Court states what it holds to be true, 'truth' is in this one stroke linguistically established. In similar fashions, the Court determines the limits of what is or is not a violation, what is separate and what is distinct, and so on, thus delimiting in reality the scope of the application of laws and the manners in which legal interpretations are to be made. In these ways, the Court determines the agenda in each case and fixes boundaries. The direction which the judicial opinion will eventually take is already taking shape in this early stage.

3.2.3 Modality

Text 3 and Text 4 show the following instances of modal usage:

Table 8. Use of modals in *Reed* and *Roe*

TEXT	should	shall	can	may	will	must
3	1	1	2	2	0	2
4	1	2	3	12	1	2

As was noted before, the use of "must", expressing the moral and legal obligation that the judicial speaker pronounces on its audience, occurs in all texts except for Text 2 (*Muller*). For example,

(11) A classification "*must* be reasonable, not arbitrary, and *must* rest upon some ground of difference having a fair and substantial relation to the object of the legislation…." (Text 3)

> (12) The woman's privacy is no longer sole and any right of privacy she possesses *must* be measured accordingly.

In (11), the judicial determination of what constitutes a reasonable classification and in (12), what privacy entails are circumscribed by the use of "must" with the judicial speaker specifying the standard against which these issues are to be measured.

"Can"(not) is found in the two texts in small numbers, as is also true of the other modals like "should", "shall" and "will". The modal "may" however is worth a special note because it is used so extensively in Text 4 (see Table 8).

Text 4 uses the highest number of deontic "may" (12 occurrences), this text being the abortion decision that was framed in terms of a discourse of rights, rather than duties and obligations. Some instances of this use of "may" in this text, however carries a meaning like "probable", i.e. the epistemic form. Some examples from Text 4 illustrate these two distinguishable uses of "may":

> (13) Maternity, or additional offspring, *may* force upon the woman a distressful life and future.

> (14) If the State is interested in protecting fetal life after viability, it *may* go so far as to proscribe abortion during that period, when it is necessary to preserve the life or health of the mother.

In (13), the meaning of "may" seems to be one of probability or likelihood. Here the Court involves itself in a predictive attitude over what may happen if freedom of choice is not allowed to the woman. In contrast, in (14), the use of "may" means "is allowable", a permission that the Court grants to the State. Hence, riding alongside this discourse of what may or may not happen, there is also the rhetoric of rights and obligations, with the Court weighing the merits and detriment of allowing the freedom of choice on the one hand and determining the nature of rights and obligations of individuals on the other.

Apart from these modal usages, there are also non-modal lexical items that index the power and authority of the Court. An example from Text 4:

> (15) There is also the distress, for all concerned, associated with the unwanted child, and there is the problem of bringing a child into a family already *unable* psychologically and otherwise, to care for it (Text 4).

Here, "unable" could be paraphrased as "lacking ability", i.e., a meaning that is expressed usually by the modal "can". Just as the Court displays its power by defining who is able and allowed to do something through the use of "can", the

Court is equally unambiguous in saying who does not have the ability (i.e. "unable") to fulfil an obligation or responsibility. We encounter once again the situation of a Court pronouncing with total confidence upon both laypersons and States alike what is or is not do-able. Such confidence comes with authority, and such authority enables it to yield power, a power that is linguistically expressed.

Once more as in the earlier texts, we witness the three aspects of the grammar of judicial texts – namely, subject-verb predication, the choice of the declarative mood, and the choice of modals (and non-modal expressions) coming together to contribute towards the differential distribution of power in the judicial opinion.

3.3 Shifts in meaning

Unlike the *Bradwell* text, Text 3 shows a more consistent use (i.e., no slippage) of "person", "parties", and "citizens". The use of these terms in this context consistently indexes both males and females. For example, in Text 3, the question of gender does not control the definition of personhood and when "person" is used, it is used in the all-inclusive sense to mean both male and female:

> (16) *Regardless of their sex, persons within any one of the enumerated classes* of that section are similarly situated with respect to that objective.

As one can tell from the explicit qualification above ("Regardless..."), the term "persons" refer to both men and women. The general absence of slippage in this text creates a more consistent treatment of males and females as equals in the eyes of the law in contrast to the situation that prevailed in Text 1.

Text 4 also discusses personhood, in the context of the exact point when life begins:

> (17) . .*no case could be cited that holds that a fetus is a person* within the meaning of the Fourteenth Amendment. The Constitution does not define "person". .in so many words. Section 1 of the Fourteenth Amendment contains three references to "person." But in nearly all. . instances, the use of the word is such that *it has application only postnatally. None indicates, with any assurance, that it has any possible pre-natal application.* All this. .persuades us that *the word "person," as used in the Fourteenth Amendment, does not include the unborn.*

The definitional restriction on the meaning of "person" to apply "only postnatally" and not any earlier directs the Court's decision to reject the contention that abortion be made illegal on the grounds of protecting potential life. Since the foetus is ruled to be *not* a person in the eyes of the Court, the argument for its protection is thus left without a solid foundation. This example provides an excellent illustration of the power of naming (in this case, "The woman is a person" versus "The foetus is not a person"), or what Bakhtin calls the "semantic authority" exerted by the author on the object (Bakhtin 1929: 164). The contrast between how personhood was defined in 1872 in *Bradwell* (namely, *not* female, or simply male) and how it is used a hundred years later in 1973 in *Roe* (i.e., postnatally, which means gender is no longer the primary or controlling issue) and beyond shows the change in the direction in the Supreme Court's treatment of gender and personhood.

Three other terms, "physician", "man's knowledge", and "privacy" found in Text 4 are also worthy of note. Under the pressure of the nineteenth century ideology of separate spheres for the sexes, there seems to be a general tendency in the judicial text to lean in favour of the male whenever there is a case of contentious semantic usage. One such case in Text 1 (*Bradwell*) has already been alluded to: words like "person" start out as an all-inclusive label and then swiftly slip into an exclusive linguistic reference for the male. What is less straightforward are instances of so-called generic uses of certain terms which can be found in Text 4. Justice Blackmun's opinion includes the following statements:

> (18) When those trained in the respective disciplines of medicine, philosophy, and theology are unable to arrive at any consensus, the judiciary, at this point in the development of *man's knowledge*, is not in a position to speculate as to the answer. . This means. .that. .the attending *physician* in consultation with *his patient*, is free to determine, without regulation by the State, that, in *his medical judgment* the patient's pregnancy should be terminated.

In the judicial writing process itself, the choice for adopting certain terms as generic (e.g., 'he' to refer to both sexes) is a decision that is currently left to the individual writer. I will not say that Blackmun's textual choices of generic pronouns and references such as "man's knowledge" rather than the more neutral phrase "human knowledge" and the use of "his" to co-index "physician" are motivated by a sexist orientation, but the fact that such choices are actually made suggests a linguistic practice that still operates from the point of view of male norms. My point is that there are various potential linguistic choices that are available to the judicial writer, and the fact that the choice 'male as generic' is exercised rather than, say, choosing to employ more inclusive language reveals the character of the authorial perspective. In my view, this practice of using male terms as generic also suggests the general reluctance in the legal context, or at least the lack of awareness on the part of lawmakers and interpreters of laws, to acknowledge explicitly the problems of accepting the male as normative.

A final example that illustrates the changes effected at the level of meaning is the extension made to the right of privacy in Text 4. Justice Blackmun's arguments proceed in the following manner: privacy is not mentioned as a right in the Constitution, but liberty is. Since freedom of choice is fundamental and since freedom has been granted to various aspects of private human relations (such as decisions involving contraception, marriage, etc.), then the abortion decision is also a privacy issue that must be protected as a fundamental right. Hence, Justice Blackmun writes:

> (19) This right of privacy, whether it be founded in the Fourteenth Amendment's concept of liberty and restrictions upon state action, as we feel it is, or, as the District Court determined, in the Ninth Amendment's reservation of rights to the people, is broad enough to encompass a woman's decision whether or not to terminate her pregnancy (Text 4).

This extension of the concept of liberty to encompass the right of privacy, and subsequent extension of this right to privacy to the abortion decision is crucial in providing the grounds for the protection of this newly defined right. The linguistic construction of rights is clearly apparent here as old meanings are broadened and recast as rights and these rights are in turn broadened and extended in new directions of application. In Text 4 then, we see an explicit instance of how new knowledge is constructed.

3.4 Resources, choices, and ground rules: The process of discursive shifts

3.4.1 The arguments and their socio-political contexts

Justice Burger, writing on behalf of a full Court in *Reed*, upheld an old ruling that:

> (20) A classification "must be reasonable, not arbitrary, and must rest upon some ground of difference having a fair and substantial relation to the object of the legislation, so that *all persons similarly circumstanced shall be treated alike.*" Royster Guano Co. v. Virginia .... (1920) (Text 3)

Where difference was once emphasized, sameness (hence, equal opportunity and access for "all persons similarly circumstanced") is invoked in Text 3, through the image constructed by the idea of similarly situated persons, male *and* female. This assimilationist thesis (i.e., one that emphasizes sameness) has the effect not only of placing both males and females in the same structural position, it also erases all gender differences as legally irrelevant. This presentation of the sexes as ungendered selves constitutes the making of a legal fiction which views both males and females *as if* gender does not exist as a dividing line, i.e, as if gender does not make any real difference. In other words, while the earlier justices on the Court adopted the view that treats gender as exerting totalizing effects, the later Courts told quite a different story – a story of ungendered beings (Schultz 1992), where difference does not matter.

Instead of placing the burden of proof on women, the central argument in Text 4 (*Roe*) details the unfair burdens that would be imposed on women should their rights to make choices in their own lives be denied:

> (21) The detriment that the State would impose upon the pregnant woman by denying this choice altogether is apparent. Specific and direct harm medically diagnosable even in early pregnancy may be involved. Maternity, or additional offspring, may force upon the woman a distressful life and future. Psychological harm may be imminent. Mental and physical health may be taxed by child care. There is also the distress, for all concerned, associated with the unwanted child, and there is the problem of bringing a child into a family already unable, psychologically and otherwise, to care for it. In other cases, as in this one, the additional difficulties and continuing stigma of unwed motherhood may be involved (Text 4).

The argument in Text 4 is cast heavily in terms of the varied effects, characterized as harms and distress, of a choice denied. In addition, the Court demands in this case that the State justifies its own laws by proving its own "compelling interest" for depriving a woman the right of choice. Thus the burden of proof, once placed squarely on women's shoulders in the past, is now lifted from women and transferred to the State.

Thus, the Courts have moved quite significantly from the days when gender exerts an essentializing and totalizing influence on defining the social roles for both men and women to the present moment where gender has become a category (like race) that is scrutinized and even deemed irrelevant in some circumstances when deciding on rights entitlements and so on. We need, however, to add the qualification that gender is in many senses still not completely on a par with race as a classification that is subject to strict scrutiny. Still, where past Courts underscored privilege when they discussed women's participation in the public sphere, more contemporary Courts increasingly employ the language of rights, coupled with a continual redefinition of what those rights are. In short, one set of discourses (of essentialism) has been replaced by a new set of discourses (of women's rights). Instead of "the law of the Creator" and "woman's physical structure", the new discourses seem to focus increasingly on the constitutional protection of rights and equality under the law, these discourses being complicated further by the constant struggle within the Court to define the meaning and the scope of these terms. Such changes in judicial rhetoric reflect the ideological movement away from a separate sphere doctrine to that which recognizes gender equality as an important dimension in social relations. The changes in the rhetoric of the Courts are thus clearly discernible.

3.4.2 Judicial styles

In terms of judicial styles, Text 3 applies the goal of the Equal Protection Clause to the specific context of *Reed:*

> (22) To give a mandatory preference to members of either sex over members of the other, merely to accomplish the elimination of hearings on the merits, is to make the very kind of arbitrary legislative choice forbidden by the Equal Protection Clause of the Fourteenth Amendment; and whatever may be said to the positive values of avoiding intrafamily controversy, the choice in this context may not lawfully be mandated solely on the basis of sex (Text 3).

By privileging this particular reading of what equal protection means and what it forbids and allows under specific circumstances, the Court prepares the grounds for striking down the Idaho statute as legally offensive to the spirit of equal protection doctrines. In Text 4, two modes are employed – namely, the doctrinal and the textual modes of argumentation:

> (23) The Constitution does not explicitly mention any right of privacy. In a line of decisions,. .the Court has recognized that a right of personal privacy, or a certain areas of zones of privacy, does exist under the Constitution. . This right of privacy. . is broad enough to encompass a woman's decision whether or not to terminate her pregnancy .

As Bobbitt observed with regard to the *Roe* opinion, "the Court asserts the doctrinal argument that the constitutional right of privacy has been established by case law" (1982: 157). Taking precedents involving issues such as interracial marriages and contraception, among others, to establish the right to personal privacy, this right is then textually applied to the abortion issue. Hence, the mode or modes of argument employed by the judicial author determines to a large extent the direction in which the arguments of the Court proceed, thus attesting to the importance and relevance of specific judicial styles in moulding the process of judicial reasoning.

3.4.3 The use of precedents

In *Reed*, the case of *Royster Guano Co. v. Virginia* (1920) is cited as the precedent that established the equal treatment of all persons who are "similarly circumstanced" (*Royster*, p.415), a principle that is used as the basis for recognizing the right of females similarly situated with males to administer an estate. Citing *Royster* therefore established for the Court and all parties concerned the long-standing principle of fairness in the law.

Shepard's Citations (1994: 1.7: 267–272) listed close to five full pages of citing cases for *Reed*. Since the same points can be made with regard to the use of precedents, I illustrate with just one such case, *Faruki v. Rogers* (1972), which is one of many cases that followed *Reed* as a precedent in arriving at its conclusions.

The case of *Faruki* centred on a statute which imposes a minimum requirement of ten years of citizenship in the United States before a naturalized citizen can serve as an officer in the Foreign Service. A three-judge District Court ruled that this ten-year requirement does not satisfy the Court's standard of compelling state interests and hence the Court ruled in favour of the plaintiff. In his opinion, Judge Wright pronounced the following statement (*Faruki* (1972): 734):

> (24) The fact that a sweeping employment qualification may have some support in the broad run of cases is often sufficient to uphold it across the board. . However, it is impossible to ignore the contrary intimations of *Reed v. Reed*. .There, in applying the restrained standard of equal protection review . ., Mr. Chief Justice Burger's opinion for a unanimous Supreme Court indicated that automatic preferences for state-granted kinds of employment could not be based purely on a feature over which a person has had no control. .I find this logic equally compelling here where, as in *Reed*, there is no proffered factual basis, except apparently blind assumption, supporting the exclusionary classification at issue.

Faruki thus adopted the reasoning in *Reed*, striking down the legality of a classification that is "based purely on a feature over which a person has had no control" (i.e., gender in *Reed*, and length of citizenship in *Faruki*), citing the latter as identical in principle with the former. In granting a similar ruling, the Court displayed its consistency in judgement and also established the legitimacy of such appeals to inter-textual authority.

The case of *Roe v. Wade* (1973) is one of the most controversial cases and continues to be among the most hotly debated cases in American legal history. The continued challenges that *Roe* faces to this day testify that such an issue is not necessarily resolved with the publication of a judicial opinion. For this reason, I discuss the precedents related to *Roe* in more detail to show that the discursive uses of precedents, whether to reaffirm or to challenge, are indeed varied. In addition to the varied nature of the precedents used, the clashes between conflicting ideologies and the shifts in ideologies that are reflected in the appeal to certain precedents will be highlighted.

The *Roe* opinion cites many precedents to lay the path for its own arguments. For example, going as far back as the 1890s, *Union Pacific Railway Co. v. Botsford* (1891) is cited by the Court to establish that the right to the control of one's own person is a sacred right that is not to be taken lightly. In *Botsford,* a passenger sued the railroad company for injuries that she sustained from a falling berth. The company, in response, demanded that she submitted to a medical examination to verify her claims. The Court ruled however that no person could be compelled to submit to such an order. In the Court's arguments, the privacy of the body and its protection from unwanted invasion are the key issues in the case. Justice Gray's opinion expressed this judgement as follows (*Botsford*, p.251):

> (25) No right is held more sacred, or is more carefully guarded, by the common law, than the right of every individual to the possession and control of his [or her] own person, free from all restraint or interference of others, unless by clear and unquestionable authority of law.

Justice Blackmun's citation of the above ruling as a precedent lays the groundwork from which the privacy arguments in *Roe* proceed. Such a choice of a precedent is crucial simply because it defines the discursive point of departure for the *Roe* decision, i.e., that "the right of every individual to the possession and control of his [or her] own person, free from all restraint or interference of others", reflecting at the same time the ideology from which the Court (the majority members of the Court, at least) operated – an ideology that privileges individual sanctity over state power to enforce its rules. Had a totally different precedent been cited instead, the starting point of the discourse would have been shifted to quite a different plane and into quite a different universe of discourse and for that reason, that sort of move would have created a totally separate web of meanings. If this had been the case, the conclusion arrived at for *Roe* might be very different from the one we know today. In short, the choice of precedents is a crucial discourse strategy, defining the discourse development in important ways.

Roe also cites *Eisenstadt v. Baird* (1972), among many other cases. *Eisenstadt* arose from the case of a Massachusetts doctor who was convicted of violating a statutory prohibition that disallows registered physicians from distributing contraceptive devices to people who are unmarried. The Court ruled in this case that (*Eisenstadt*, p.453):

> (26) If under *Griswold* the distribution of contraceptives to married persons cannot be prohibited, a ban on distribution to unmarried persons would be equally impermissible. . If the right of privacy means anything, it is the right of the individual, married or single, to be free from unwarranted governmental intrusion into matters so fundamentally affecting a person as the decision whether to bear or beget a child.

Griswold v. Connecticut (1965), also cited in *Roe*, legalizes the use of contraceptives for married people on the grounds of the protected privacy of the family unit. *Eisenstadt* extended this privacy further by arguing in favour of protecting the privacy of unmarried individuals. Against this backdrop of a more liberal definition of privacy that frowned on governmental or other external interferences, the decision in *Roe* takes shape. Privacy, in *Roe*, is said to extend to the individual's decision regarding the abortion decision, or more accurately, the right to the decision whether or not to terminate a pregnancy. Putting questions about the sanctity of life aside, what perhaps makes this case all the more controversial or problematic is that the individuals involved in such decisions relevant here are *women*. Given that the question of women and their right to power and control has been an issue of public debate since time immemorial, a case that involves a question of whether or not to assign the right to control to women themselves becomes a highly charged issue, with potential conflicts arising from all sides. In this sense then, *Roe* is not just a case about gender issues but is also about the problematics of gender and power like in all the other cases that I have considered here.

Shepard's Citations (1994: 1.7: 588–598) yields a very long list of citations for *Roe* (ten-and-a-half pages to be exact). Here, I give a taste of two such citations. One is *Rosen v. Louisiana State Board of Medical Examiners* (1974).

Rosen involved a doctor who was charged with violating a statute that holds a person liable for helping to procure an abortion. The doctor's licence was suspended in the case, and an appeal to a three-judge district court to review the constitutionality of the statute failed to bring about the desired outcome. The Supreme Court, upon review, later reversed the district court's decision. With respect to the *Roe* ruling, the district court conceded that (*Rosen*, p.877):

> (27) The United States Supreme Court is the final arbiter of constitutional guarantees and having passed on this issue, the Court has foreclosed any reconsideration by us.

In the concurrence to this opinion, the same court further added (p.878):

> (28) The Supreme Court's decisions in *Roe* and *Doe*, *supra*, are in fundamental opposition to the majority opinion which we wrote in this case pertaining to the anti-abortion provision of the Louisiana Medical Practice Act when it was first before us. We have no alternative now but to follow the Supreme Court decisions on abortion which are the supreme law of the land.

The reluctance with which the *Roe* (and *Doe)* decision is accepted as law should be easily discernible. It is also appropriate to note at this point that the two justices who dissented in *Roe*, Justices Byron White and William Rehnquist, also made the following statement in the context of the Louisiana case discussed here. Justice White, joined by Justice Rehnquist, writes this special note to the Louisiana case (p.1098):

> (29) Under the compulsion of *Roe v. Wade, 410 U.S. 113 (1973)*, and *Doe v. Bolton, 410 U.S. 179 (1973)*, which in my view were erroneously decided, I join the affirmance.

The discursive challenges to the *Roe* decision are numerous, the examples given here being simply a small drop in the ocean of protests over it. These challenges are testimonies to the competing and conflicting ideologies that exist in certain factions within the Supreme Court itself and in the lower courts, and not just among members of the general public. There are however also many instances where *Roe* is cited positively. *Planned Parenthood of Central Missouri v. Danforth* (1976) is just one such case.

In *Danforth*, the *Roe* decision is cited to show that there is in fact no inconsistency between the two cases, and in that gesture of 'harmonizing' (*Shepard's* terminology), the two cases support each other. *Danforth* explored the issue of the viability of the foetus, among others, where there was said to be a clash in the definition of viability as established by the Missouri statute and the *Roe* opinion. In his concurring opinion, Justice Stewart downplayed the discrepancies and harmonized the alleged difference in the following way (*Danforth*, p.89):

> (30) With respect to the definition of viability in 2(2) of the Act, it seems to me that the critical consideration is that the statutory definition has almost no operative significance. . I do not believe it conflicts with the statement in *Roe v. Wade*. .

In this way, challenges to *Roe* are avoided through a discursive resolution of potential conflicts effected in the written opinions of the judges.

4. Summary

From the analysis of *Reed* and *Roe*, it should be clearly discernible that there is indeed a shift in the judicial rhetoric since the *Bradwell* era. The earlier rhetoric made gender out to be a crucial determinant of woman's place and roles, and these are in turn used to rationalize and justify women's exclusion from participation in the public sphere. In *Reed* and *Roe*, woman's personhood status is recognized and affirmed and gender as a legitimate basis for denying women their place in public life comes under stricter judicial scrutiny. The power of judicial discourse to determine woman's place in American society through its definition of women's rights and privileges is thus immense. Whether the Court and its judicial players choose to affirm public/popular opinion or to shape American society by effecting new alternative discourses that replace existing rhetoric and which change the direction of court decisions is something that I have argued here to be within the power of judges, particularly Supreme Court judges.

CHAPTER 5

Of equality and justice

Language, gender, and legal ideology in the American context

> Axes of social difference are potentially axes of power, and the distribution of that power, especially the power to be heard, is, as Bourdieu reminds us, by no means guaranteed or justly distributed. . I believe that all discourse is situated, that it occurs in a historical context, that its creation and reception are marked with the traces of the life histories of all participants. . To forget them is to encourage us to ignore them, to offer the false comfort of forgetting these facts; in short, it is not to contest existing ideologies. It is to pretend that everyone else has ideologies, but we, as academics, as social scientists, as students of language, do not or that these ideologies do not extend to our preferred forms of discourse or objects of study. After all, what is entitlement except the luxury of an unreflecting assumption that other humans, equally rational, would, when faced with a given situation, make the same choice we would make for exactly the same reasons?
>
> –Keith Walters (1995:6)

1. From analysis to real life: Lessons from the analysis

The linguistic choices that are made in the production of judicial discourse can be viewed as motivated choices, at times reflecting individual agendas and at other times reflecting institutional ground rules. Each term in the judges' vocabulary, we may argue has been chosen, whether the judges are conscious of it or not, to cohere with the point of view of the Court, and at the individual level, with the personal ideology of the judicial speaker/writer.

As many scholars will agree, ideology works best when its presence is unobtrusive. The predominance of indirect indexical relations thus contributes to the covert nature of the ideologies in the judicial discourse I have examined in this book. It must be remembered that 'covert' is not to be equated with a lack of power. On the contrary, it is precisely the fact that the ideology that pervades the discourse is so insidiously and skilfully woven into the discourse that makes the power in the discourse so real. Such a discursive naturalization of particular ideological viewpoints contributes to the control of particular definitions of 'reality'. The Whorfian idea of habitual thought as a key influence on one's worldview is of relevance here. Indeed, Whorf's notion of the linguistic determination of thought is perhaps best understood at the discourse level than at the level of the language system.

The changes that individual words and phrases have undergone are illustrated by semantic shifts, resulting in shifting indexical referents, found in the use of words such as "person" and "privacy". As the Court's ideas of what constitute personhood and privacy are transformed through the course of American social and political history, the legal institution reflects these changes in the wider social and political context by narrowing and widening the scope of personhood and privacy from case to case. In short, how words are used and defined and what they are stipulated to mean at the level of language play a very important role in defining the rights and legal status of individuals at the level of society and culture. Through the Court's particular creations of very special lexical meaning relationships, the legal institution defines the roles of individuals in society. It is in this crucial sense that the relationship between signs and their (social) referents is argued to be an ideologically motivated and not an arbitrary one.

The systematic nature of the lexical patterning in inscribing institutional rules and social roles is further elaborated at the level of grammar. The grammatical patterning between authoritative subjects and verbs on the one hand, and that between powerless subjects and verbs on the other, serve to reinforce the differential distribution of power in the judicial setting. Thus, plaintiffs and defendants can only take on the roles that are designated by the Court and they have to accept the judgements handed down by the justices as final and binding. Justices, in contrast, are free, relatively speaking at least, to dictate and to pronounce their decisions on those who come before them to plead their cases. The grammatical patterning in the judicial discourse therefore linguistically parallel the social standings and the hierarchical structure of the political economy, as exemplified microcosmically in the court culture that is manifested in the judicial opinions. The power of these linguistic patterns is further underscored by the Court's use of the declarative mood, coupled with Court statements delivered in an authoritative, monologic style, and by the choice of particular modals. The co-presence of the declarative mood, strong modals and performative-style verbs has the effect of positioning the Court as an active and legitimate agent with the rights to pronounce statements on ordinary citizens, who must, in their turn, act in accordance with the Court's rulings. Though the linguistic resources are, at the theoretical level, available to all users, it is clear that only a select group of users may choose to realize certain choices in the appropriate settings. The grammar of judicial discourse illustrates precisely this: only judges can make declarations and these declarations come in the form of powerful speech acts whose force is unmistakable. In this triple convergence of grammatical patterning, pragmatic power and semantic authority in judicial discourse, the power of judges, of courts, and of the ideologies which inform their actions are consolidated and are continuously reinforced.

The significance of shifts in meanings in the terms of discourse, linguistic or otherwise, is that they testify to the fluidity of signification and the authority of the speaker/writer. That an individual (such as a judge), suitably legitimated with power and authority, can define how words mean through an act of saying is perhaps one of the most powerful examples we can hope to find of performative usage. Hence, that personhood is defined in a certain way (namely, as male) at a certain time but defined another way at another time (i.e., with only postnatal applications) is due largely to the semantic authority that society allocates to courts, though it must be acknowledged that society itself must sustain the right climate for such a linguistic move, thus making society both the allocator of meanings and an accomplice to upholding what meanings will be made relevant at a particular time. This is *not* to say that courts and society work always in tandem with each other, for often, the direction that courts take may actually be "out of step with the public mood" (Greenhouse 1995b). As Greenhouse recently notes, "Such disharmony is scarcely surprising, as Justices with life tenure often outlast not only the presidents who appointed them but also the entire political era in which they joined the Court". However, this is also not to say that agreement is never found between the views of the courts and those of the society. Through naming and signification then, the Court carves out a linguistic reality that may find agreement with certain sections of society while at the same time may not be endorsed by other sections. But whatever version of 'reality' is constructed by the Court, the Court's move has the consequence of defining and constructing a new social reality that translates into an individual's roles and a person's rights. Underlying these acts of shifting significations is an accompanying movement of changing ideologies and socio-political values, the latter acting to sustain the climate for linguistic shifts and, at the same moment, to be reaffirmed and constituted by the shifts in usage. In short, where the linguistic forms are, the ideology is never far behind.

Beyond the level of lexis, grammar, semantics and pragmatics is the judicial employment of the standard language. The voices of judges are presented to the public in the form of a standard language, this being an index of the judges' social and political prestige derived from their being members of an elite. The choice of a standard language expresses an ideology that "is part of a greater power construct, a set of social practices on which people depend without close analysis of underlying assumptions" (Lippi-Green 1994: 166). Hence, the use of standard language keys into a power network that is at once recognizable by members of society, including those on the lower part of the social hierarchy, and often the choice goes unquestioned, even by those who do not identify with it. Given the generally uncritical acceptance of standard language as a mark of social prestige, the voice of the Court, dressed in standard forms, thus comes through as legitimate and authoritative and in this way, the pragmatic power of the judiciary is further enhanced.

The salient features that emerge from my analysis of the different levels of linguistic patterning testify to two important points. Firstly, though I will not claim that any one feature in judicial discourse indicates any kind of intentional or conscious workings of a dominant ideology, it seems clear that the confluence of different factors converging within the same stretch of discourse cannot be dismissed as totally arbitrary or fortuitous. Instead, the intersection of the linguistic patterns at several levels of analysis should raise our suspicion to the possibility of the specific workings of an institutional ideology. Thus, the semantic authority inherent in the linguistic definitions of terms, the dominance of verbs of saying, the overwhelming presence of the declarative mood and the monologic style of court rhetoric, and so on, are consistent with the nature of an institutional ideology which directs the law, the society, and the culture.

Secondly, to show how shifts in the discourse are effected, this book has explored the influence of specific arguments, judicial styles, and the choice of precedents on the nature of each judicial opinion. The essentialization of male and female roles in the *Bradwell* and the *Muller* Courts emerge as the primary strategy that the presiding judges employed to put men and women in their 'rightful' places. An association was found between males and the public domain and between females and the private sphere, which the judges, in part with society's endorsement, defined as an inevitable consequence of human biology and natural laws. Such an overt equation with natural law and divine ordinance not only lends weight to the judicial arguments, but also functions to mask a judicial/social construction as 'truth' grounded in the 'facts' of 'human reality'. Under such a construction, men and women come before the Court with their (legal and social) status pre-defined. The Court's role under such an unchanging ideology of separate spheres seems merely one of re-affirming and confirming the dominant social and political values of the period.

Later judicial strategies shifted from making arguments based on essence to constructing a notion of equality that makes gender differences legally suspect and irrelevant. In *Reed,* for example, the effect of defining equality between the sexes based on the criterion of "similarly situated" selves is to cause the un-gendering of these selves. I argue that an equality that is defined in a manner that says gender does not matter is itself a legal fiction in the same way that essentialism was once upheld as 'truth'. In my view, even present-day America cannot lay claim to having so effective a policy of equal protection that it generates similarly situated individuals, with no regard for race, gender, and economic power. The fact of the matter is that each of us comes with a gender, a race, a social position, and an ideology that is potentially in conflict with other ideologies. Even within the narrow context of *Reed*, the ideas of similarly situated individuals and similar treatment are problematic as they assume agreement where none might exist. The Court's treatment of gender or race as irrelevant is thus yet another legal fiction of justice that only reflects a different, but an equally constructed, ideological position.

Each judicial strategy therefore facilitates and rationalizes the Court's arguments for directing the decisions one way rather than another. The strategies that the Court uses change with the socio-historical and discursive climate in which the Court is itself embedded. Hence, essentialism cannot be a conceivable argument in the post-*Reed* era, and conversely, the equality thesis would not be a plausible or possible argument to employ in the earlier courts, even if it had been available then, given the more conservative social and legal climate characteristic at that point in American history when Blackstone's exhortation of a separate-sphere philosophy still ruled the thinking of most. But as the analysis and discussion move from one judicial opinion to another, it becomes clear that the shifts effected in the discourse, either by redefining old terms in new ways or by inventing new terms (or new fictions), help to bridge the social and historical transitions which brought American society and culture through each period. As old meanings are ignored, contested or simply replaced and infused with new significances, new knowledge is forged directly at the site of these discursive battles for dominance. The choices that were made and the ones that won the day are influenced by the varied personalities, individual beliefs and ideologies that met head-on with the institutional pressures, public sentiments and local and national politics. Each judicial opinion is thus unique in the way it bears and reflects the marks of particular influences that shape its production.

Gal (1989, 1991) has observed that linguistic forms have no power in themselves, but reflect the power of the group they index. While I have no problems with such a statement, I will nonetheless add that when these 'innocent' linguistic forms fall into the hands of those who command power, these forms are potentially capable of being transformed into (powerful) speech acts. The judicial opinion comprises a series of speech acts, each one dictating what litigants should or should not do. Under these circumstances, it becomes actually difficult to separate the forms from the power of the group indexed by these forms, thus illustrating in a most compelling way both the power inherent in discourse and the discourse of power, as well as their complex relations.

The benefits that one can discern from a detailed treatment of judicial discourse are several. Paying attention to the individual discourse in its context helps one to see how the set of linguistic, social, political and cultural meanings that are indexed by it came to be possible and even meaningful within its own matrix. Examining a whole set of discourses across the history of a culture further enriches this understanding by filling in the synchronic gaps as we move diachronically over time. The movements in the discourse provide us with a sense of the drifts and changes in the values and ideologies of the society under scrutiny. Understanding these changes in turn enables us to appreciate the need for context, the importance of political economy, and the power of linguistic and social constructions.

A multidisciplinary approach shows that past and contemporary debates about discourse, gender, power and ideology necessarily extend beyond the concerns of any one discipline. A multidisciplinary perspective raises our awareness that the analysis of discourse, gender politics and ideology must be located in the context of a wider economy of scholarship, since these are all issues that do not stop short at exerting only local repercussions. Rather, they implicate an entire political economy. In short, current debates in any of these issues must always take into consideration both their immediate and wider contexts.

2. Gender (in)equalities and gender justice: Continuing dialogues of contemporary relevance

As Kay (1988: 1) observes, "[t]he notion that men and women stand as equals before the law was not the original understanding". Due to its common-law heritage that suspended the married woman's legal existence through coverture, for most of the nineteenth century and the opening decades of the twentieth century, America embraced the separate-sphere doctrine that kept the sexes separate and unequal. Proponents of the equality thesis were shocked to find that even within the wording of the Fourteenth Amendment to the Constitution, which is one of the amendments that specifically seeks to establish the constitutional guarantee of equality, the word "male" is used in the same breath as "persons" and "citizens". It is thus not surprising that in an earlier era when constitutional protection for women as a group was unheard of, in the case of *Bradwell v. Illinois (1872)*, the issue of personhood, specifically aligning "person" with "male" became a crucial ground for the argument against the inclusion of females in an all-male profession.

When Myra Bradwell stood before the courts to argue for her right to engage in an occupation of her choice, she stood before the justices as a citizen of the United States. Hence, when the lower courts first ruled against her on account of her sex, she vehemently described the court's decision as an annihilation of rights (*Chicago Legal News*, February 5, 1870, cited in Friedman 1993: 21):

> What the decision of the Supreme Court of the United States in the Dred Scot case was to the rights of the negroes as citizens of the U.S., this decision is to the political rights of women in Illinois – annihilation.

When she appealed to the Supreme Court, she was essentially told by the Court that being female and being a lawyer were not compatible notions. The (restrictive) linguistic definition for "person" was thus applied in a way that was in agreement with the prevailing ideology of separate and unequal social and legal positions for the sexes.

Myra Bradwell was certainly not alone in encountering such an overt exclusion. In 1894, Belva Lockwood encountered similar oppositions when she applied to the Virginia bar. After overcoming various obstacles, Lockwood was granted her right to practise in the District of Columbia in 1873 and subsequently in 1879, she became the first woman to practise before the United States Supreme Court (Hoff 1991: 183). These honours, however, were still viewed as insufficient. The Supreme Court of Appeals of Virginia refused to admit Lockwood by invoking the same argument that only men were "persons" eligible for legal practice in Virginia. This exclusionary policy is in opposition to a Supreme Court judgement two decades before that established women as persons (*Minor v. Happersett, 88 U.S. (21 Wall.) 162, 1874*, a case involving suffrage rights). The historical and legal significance of *Lockwood* is, as Hoff notes, that the federal court chose to allow states a narrower interpretation of the meaning of "person" (1991: 184), thus continuing to limit female participation outside the home.

Public participation by women was thus extensively curbed in the late nineteenth century in America either by a narrow construction of personhood or by an outright denial of the right to vote. This trend of female exclusion from the public realm continues well into the twentieth century. I will resume this discussion of the concept of "person" with particular regard to *Roe v. Wade (1973)* in a short while. A brief review here on the contemporary state of women's participation in the law will show the implications and repercussions of restrictive female participation in the law, which resulted from a legacy of the separate and unequal thesis, are still felt today.

In 1922, a woman who contemplated going to law school said (cited in Kay 1988: 880):

> At the time, I was ready to enter law school, women were looked upon as people who should not be in law schools. .I wanted very much to go to Columbia, but I couldn't get in. I went over to see Harlan Stone, Dean Stone, who was later Chief Justice, and asked him to open the law school [to women] and he said no. . I asked him why. .and he said "We don't because we don't." That was final.

Other law schools throughout the nation held a similar attitude towards potential female law students. Harvard Law School, for example, did not open its doors to women till the 1950s (Kay 1988: 880). In fact, it was not till the end of 1970 that the Association of American Law Schools took steps to bar sex discrimination in admissions and employment policies (Kay 1988: 880). The nation's highest Court, as is now common knowledge, did not include a woman on its bench until 1981 when Justice Sandra Day O'Connor was appointed. In 1992, there were only thirteen female law school deans in the United States, four of whom had announced their resignations by May 1994 (Kay 1994: 390). In short, though American women presently have access to the nation's law schools and to legal practice an entire century after *Bradwell*, the figures showed in study after study that their entry into the profession is still met with obstacles, especially for women of colour (see Delgado and Bell 1989). These, I argue, are the effects of the power of the linguistic and ideological constructions of social realities in which particular ideologies (e.g., female exclusion) were upheld and made to seem a part of the 'natural' order of things. Women have been kept separate and confined within the private sphere for so long that their access to the public realm is only now made possible; even so, this access is still a highly problematic one to this day (see Drachman 1998 for more details on this subject).

In the early years of the twentieth century, cases involving unequal treatment in the law based solely on sex continued to define American constitutional history. In places where a total ban on women's participation in the public sphere had proven difficult to enforce, specific statutes were enacted to restrict the nature and the extent of this participation. Thus, the Supreme Court's affirmation of an Oregon statute which determined the maximum number of hours in which Mrs Gotcher can work outside the home in its ruling in *Muller v. Oregon (1908)* is an example of such a restriction placed on women. In making this ruling, the Court ignored its own precedential ruling in *Lochner v. New York (1905)*, where it was argued that setting maximum hours of work violated a male or female citizen's liberty to freely contract with employers. The *Muller* decision was based on the supposed weakness of the female constitution to endure long hours of work (*outside* the home), a weakness that was said to be grounds for special legal 'protection'.

In a similar case in New York in 1924, a woman was convicted of violating a statute which banned employment of women in city restaurants between the hours of ten in the evening and six in the morning, the reasons cited being the dangers of the city and the irreversible effects of sleep deprivation that will adversely affect women's health (*Radice v. New York, 264 U.S. 292*). Further, in 1948, the case of *Goesaert v. Cleary* upheld a Michigan statute which disallowed a woman from working as a bartender (a more lucrative position) unless she was related to the male owner of the bar, again citing the special protection of women against the 'immoral' and 'violence-prone' atmosphere prevalent in bars. It was as late as 1971 that one court, the California Supreme Court, finally lifted the ban on women serving as bartenders, hence placing women on an equal footing with their male colleagues (*Sail'er Inn, Inc. v. Kirby*).

All these cases illustrate the different ways in which varied restrictions were placed on female participation, making it either not economically viable or overtly difficult for women to exercise their choices fully. The restrictions that were imposed were based on social constructions of women's presumed frailty, which then affirmed the ideologically constructed interpretations of constitutional protection and confinement within certain realms. Unfortunately, such restrictions are still evident everywhere to this day; the various challenges against the abortion law established in *Roe v. Wade (1973)* testify to this fact.[1] As long as these restrictions are legitimated by law itself, women cannot hope to become full members of society with the same rights that are accorded to men. In this sense, gender inequalities and injustices are as much in our midst now as they were the realities of women's lives in the past. Maintaining and legitimating ideologies of separateness between the sexes can thus only mean unreasonable exclusion and unequal treatment in the law.

In 1961, a challenge was tendered against a Florida law that failed to require women to serve on juries in the same way that it required men to serve *(Hoyt v. Florida, 368 U.S. 57, 1961*). Gwendolyn Hoyt charged that due to this statute, she was denied a jury of her (female) peers, thus effectively biasing the trial for second-degree murder against her. Reinforcing the age-old belief that "woman is still the center of home and family life", the Supreme Court ruled that the Florida statute was *not* unconstitutional as charged, and so Gwendolyn Hoyt was convicted of second-degree murder by the all-male jury. Interestingly, this very same question of the (gendered) process of jury selection was raised once more in 1975 (*Taylor v. Louisiana, 419 U.S. 522, 1975)* and again in a more recent case, *J.E.B. v. Alabama (1994)*, but in both these cases, *men* brought forward the lawsuits, and both, I may add, were successful in their challenges.

The turning point for American women came in 1971, when Sally Reed brought a gender discrimination suit before the United States Supreme Court. As Hoff has noted, with the *Reed* decision, "the Supreme Court invalidated *for the first time in its history* a state statute on the grounds of sex discrimination" (1991: 247, emphasis in original). A classification, as the Court finally acknowledged, must be "reasonable, not arbitrary, and must rest upon some ground of difference having a fair and substantial relation to the object of the legislation, so that all persons similarly circumstanced shall be treated alike" (*Royster*

Guano Co. v. Virginia, 253 U.S. 412, 1920).[2] In whatever manner one prefers to interpret the implications of the *Reed* decision, it is clear that for the first time in American legal history, the high Court has finally taken more serious notice of constitutional challenges involving gender discrimination. The ideology of separate spheres has thus, on the surface at least, finally been replaced by one that favours equal treatment for the sexes.[3] This shift in ideology has taken more than a century to be effected, and as the many cases that continue to be brought before the Supreme Court show, the shift towards some form of equality is far from complete.

Despite the inadequacies of the 1971 decision, it must be acknowledged that without *Reed*, the victory claimed by subsequent cases may not have been possible. In *Roe v Wade (1973),* for example, the rhetoric of liberation in this abortion rights case would not have been possible without a prior establishment of the discourse of equality and rights. Unlike the abortion debate in post-socialist Hungary where abortion is "less linked to sexuality and women's autonomy" (Gal 1994:284) but linked more directly to questions of national identity and human rights, in the United States, the issue seems to be one that is more centrally located in an ethics of morality and a battle of individual freedom of choice.

The issue of personhood and personal rights once again raises its head, as it did in the late nineteenth century. At one time, "person" means "only male," in *Roe*, "person" is said to apply "only postnatally". This difference in the linguistic definition of personhood makes all the difference in *Roe* as potential life is opposed to the interests of the (female) person, thus paving the way for the argument that a woman's right to privacy overrides the rights of the hitherto unestablished personhood of the foetus. What the past construction of personhood denied to Myra Bradwell and Belva Lockwood, the new construction won for Jane Roe. In this example, we cannot fail to appreciate the importance of linguistic definitions and social constructions of ideas and ideologies, and how the shifting ideologies of what constitute personhood, privileges and rights guide each judicial decision.

The emotions and explosive debates that are still currently witnessed in the United States on the abortion question are indicative of the high stakes that different groups perceive to be at issue. *Roe v. Wade* has legally established the right to an abortion for American women, a fundamental right argued as associated with personal privacy, thus reinstating not only the personhood status of women but also privileging the sanctity of (female) personhood over potential life. The continual and unrelenting challenges to the decision in *Roe*, however, show that the ideology of (female) rights and (gender) equality is a long way from being the established norm.

In my view, one of the underlying issues in *Roe* is an issue of competing ideologies, power, and control. Though the abortion debate is popularly dressed in arguments of moral values and the sanctity of human life, it seems to me that at least one of the questions underlying the debates is an old one: who should control the female body? The social and political revolutions (such as granting suffrage rights to women in 1920, and the additions of various Title Acts to achieve equality in various spheres) that twentieth-century America has undergone has made it untenable to restrict women's participation in civil life beyond a certain minimal level before the restriction becomes questionable. Granted that it is not always agreed that the abortion issue is a case of gender-based discrimination, that the abortion decision directly involves women's life choices makes it suspicious that the issue should draw so much attention.[4] Subsequent cases involving control over various aspects of the reproductive process, such as *Carey v. Population Services International (1977)* on restricting the availability and distribution of contraceptive devices, *City of Akron v. Akron Center for Reproductive Health, Inc. (1983)*, which involved the regulations to be placed on the performance of abortions, and *Planned Parenthood of Southeastern Pennsylvania v. Casey (1992)*, again on enforcing restrictive measures on abortions, to name just three, are all challenges to the established right to the decisions involved in a woman's reproductive freedom. The continuing dialogues and debates since the 1973 Supreme Court ruling testify to the continued relevance and the problems surrounding the issue of what personhood and the full assertion of rights mean for women in this country. Clearly, a crucial part of the debates centres on a "pro-life" ideology versus that of pro-choice, and the social constructions of (female) personhood and the rights of (female) personhood. Among the functions that discursive strategies serve, the types of discursive strategies discussed here mask the underlying issues of hegemonic control and power distribution in contemporary American society.

It is telling that in the history of American law, what prevails in legal rhetoric is the term 'sex discrimination' and not 'gender discrimination'. The commonly asserted difference between the terms 'sex' and 'gender' is that 'sex' pertains to questions of biology, whereas 'gender' addresses issues of social and cultural constructions (see Butler 1990 for a critique of this issue).

That 'sex discrimination' should be the term used for the most parts of American legal history is thus revealing of the predilection on the law's part for essentialism with respect to gender issues, rather than to admit to the realities of socio-cultural constructions and to face up to the consequences of such constructions.

The question of gender has periodically been placed alongside the issue of race. In *Bradwell,* for example, Myra Bradwell herself provided the analogy between gender equality and racial equality, as noted earlier. Later, in *Reed,* Sally Reed made the same point in a brief submitted to the Court (cited in Kay 1988: 17, emphasis mine):

> The sex line drawn by Sec.15–314, mandating subordination of women to men without regard to individual capacity, creates a "suspect classification" requiring close judicial scrutiny. Although the legislature may distinguish between individuals on the basis of their need or ability, it is presumptively impermissible to distinguish *on the basis of an unalterable identifying trait over which the individual has no control* and for which he or she should not be disadvantaged by the law. *Legislative discrimination grounded on sex, for purposes unrelated to any biological difference between the sexes, ranks with legislative discrimination based on race, another congenital, unalterable trait of birth, and merits no greater judicial deference.*

In *J.E.B.,* which involves jury selection, gender is again brought on the same plane with race when Justice Blackmun stated in the opinion of the Court that

> [w]hile the prejudicial attitudes toward women in this country have not been identical to those held toward racial minorities, the similarities between the experiences of racial minorities and women, in some contexts, 'overpower those differences'.

It seems curious that American courts have taken so long to admit that just as race is an immutable characteristic that qualifies it as a suspect classification in the eyes of the law, gender (in biological terms) is also immutable, and thus must equally be treated as suspect whenever it is used as the only ground for exclusion. This disparity suggests that women are frequently ranked below men, regardless of race, and that though women constitute at least fifty percent (or more) in the general population, they are to be regarded as the true minority, or so to speak, the silent majority. Unfortunately, the separate and unequal thesis remains very much with us.

Though much of the rhetoric has changed through the course of time, the issues that are addressed through the ages have remained fairly constant. Thus, we find ourselves in the American context to be still debating over issues of participation, rights and equality. As the courts at certain moments grant more and more rights to minorities and women, it still seems for most people that the courts have been generally slow to accord many of these rights to women given that the legal battles for women's rights have an extensive history. It is an interesting comment on the changing times that recent cases on gender discrimination and (in)equality that have appeared to mark the landscape of American legal history were brought forth by men.

Though *J.E.B.* establishes a commitment towards fair and equal treatments in the courts, and it also hints at how American worldviews have changed through the decades to some extent, the fact that the decision reflects the majority opinion of only four justices should caution us as to how tenuous this victory is. In many ways, the gulf that divides the two sexes throughout the course of American history seems not to have been significantly bridged after all these years. In many arenas, equality still eludes women, and the rights that women have achieved in this country are still continually subject to and are ever vulnerable to challenges. As long as the sexes remain separate in spirit, equality will always be an elusive dream. However, much has certainly been achieved in the past century, and many of these achievements have been attained against seemingly insurmountable odds. For this reason, I am hopeful that even if gender justice and equality come to us at a pace that is not to our liking, these are nevertheless hopes that can be realized with continued negotiations, contestations, and perseverance both in the courts and in the public forum.

3. Crossing disciplinary borders: The discourse of the law of gender discrimination

The kind of scholarship that is produced by various disciplines or sub-fields has been motivated and directed, understandably, by very specific goals and oriented towards their own cause(s). This directedness in each field of research has unnecessarily shrunk the horizons of human knowledge as each artificially carves out its own territory and engages in the academic pursuit of problems that are most locally relevant. As a result of such a compartmentalization of knowledge, and the general lack of communication among the disciplines, scholars affiliated to different disciplines have drifted farther and farther apart from one another. The product of these drifts and the failure to communicate is that we produce knowledge that are seemingly relevant and of interest only to ourselves and to those who share our goals. In addition, the knowledge we produce are at best just that – miniscule, disconnected, and fragmented.

To avoid this kind of narrow perspective, we must promote inter- and multidisciplinary research and scholarly cooperation. It is for these reasons that in this book I have sought to utilize multiple frameworks for the study of judicial discourse, making possible an understanding of law and judicial discourse from different perspectives and showing how ideas from other disciplines may be exploited to give a richer reading of specific instances of judicial texts. In other words, multiple perspectives enable a broadening of scope in conceptualizing issues.

In his introductory paper in the book, *Reinventing Anthropology* (1969), Hymes maintains that research must meet five 'criteria': responsiveness, critical awareness, ethical concern, human relevance, and a "clear connection between what is to be done and the interests of [hu]mankind" (p.7). Using my research as a case in point, this book stresses that discourse analysis as a method of linguistic analysis must be responsive to social concerns by paying attention to language use in context. Emphasis is also placed on the need to cultivate vigilance and critical awareness in our approach to scholarship, especially in ideology research. Among the motivations that guide this book is the ethical concern for equality and justice. The specific focus on the judicial opinions, an important form of discourse of one of the principal players in the legal institution, is tendered as an answer to Hymes' call for relevance in scholarship.

The implications of a linguistically and socially constructed ideology and worldview are far-reaching and deep. To say of ideologies that they are constructed is not the same as saying that they are necessarily false and that individuals who live within the ideologies are deluded beings. All that we, as members of groups, communities, societies and cultures have to recognize is that being constructions, ideologies and worldviews represent specific interests set within particular socio-political realities of the life of every individual. By cultivating a critical awareness of the nature of ideologies, the nature of constructions, and the role of the surrounding realities of the political economy in influencing these constructions, individuals will find themselves in a better position to appreciate, understand, support, contest and resist the 'facts' of daily living.

Whatever we engage in, in whatever capacities, we must always take into account the accompanying linguistic, social, political, cultural and historical contexts that we are necessarily embedded in by virtue of the situatedness of the human condition. Just as every stretch of discourse echoes within itself the multiplicity of voices from the past and the present, every act on the individual's part presupposes previous understandings and resonates with future repercussions. Situatedness, or the need to contextualize and to be critically aware of contexts, is by no means a novel idea. However, most individuals (scholars and laypeople alike), despite their own embeddedness within systems, have not always recognized and understood the connectedness and the ideology-laden nature of their positions, or as Keith Walters says, "everyone else has ideologies, but we. .do not" (SALSA address, 1995)! Such self-reflexivity is an understanding that is worth cultivating, for what better education can we seek for ourselves than the education of ourselves, of others, our natures, and the nature of our environment?

The constant stress that I place on the situatedness and the multidisciplinary nature of research as well as on the contextualization of individual life in its relevant political economy as demonstrated by the present study of language, law, ideology, society and culture is more faithful to Fishman's call for a sociolinguistics that addresses the issue of who speaks what to who, when, where and why (Fishman 1965) than what much of modern mainstream sociolinguistics has done. By contextualizing research endeavours within relevant political economies, I believe that we have effectively progressed from a time when we were contented with doing 'socially realistic' linguistics to an era when we are increasingly accepting (and demanding) 'socially constituted' linguistics as the norm (Hymes 1972b). I hold, as Hymes (1972a) has stated before, that *a genuine theory of linguistics is a theory of language, and not merely a formal theory of grammar*. At its best, the importance of works such as this one on ideology and political economy lies in the message that the study of language (as living discourse) as a social, political and cultural phenomenon can no longer be marginalized within contemporary linguistic traditions, formal or otherwise. In short, socially constituted linguistics must be re-centred, reconstituted and returned to its rightful place – namely, at the centre of the study of living discourses.

The objective of this work goes, however, beyond re-establishing and re-affirming the importance of a basic sociolinguistic principle and the wider principle of contextualized living. Apart from its direct contributions to (socio)linguistics in showing the links between the linguistic-referential, the linguistic-social, the linguistic-political, and the linguistic-ideological, thus locating and identifying the site in discourse where different dimensions intersect, this work contributes directly to gender studies, feminist legal scholarship and critical legal studies, studies in ideology, semiotics, linguistic anthropology, and the study of political economy.

Though the issue of gender in the law has received the attention of scholars, the language of judicial opinions has not been as extensively explored by linguists. As very important and powerful players in the laws of a society, the (linguistic) behaviour of judges becomes a crucially relevant aspect of study, and certainly one that merits scholarly attention. In addition, though gender issues have by now long been appreciatively studied within the context of communities, the interplay between questions of gender, social inequalities, ideology, and the influence of the judicial culture on these issues have not been adequately addressed, at least not from the linguistic viewpoint. My work not only bridges these gaps, but also paves the way for more work into judicial discourse and the linguistic study of legal (in)equalities and gender-based discrimination.

I believe that focusing on judicial language is a fruitful angle for feminists and feminist lawyers to look more critically into the judicial language users operating within the bounds of individual and institutional ideologies. Though it is true (to some extent) that judges do not make the laws in the United States, it is nevertheless important to acknowledge that the courts play an extremely important part in reinforcing and perpetuating the laws that Congress enacts. Judges as writers, speakers, and readers are in a position to shape and interpret laws in ways that often prove significant in terms of what these laws mean for all concerned. As much of critical legal studies and feminist jurisprudence have concentrated primarily on legal theories, case studies, and legal interpretation of cases and statutes, I hope the present focus on judges and their discourse will infuse legal scholarship with a fresh way for locating the problems faced by women in encountering the law, and for appreciating the possible reasons for some of the legal successes in more recent times.

Ideology, as Bourdieu (1977) has said, is most effective when it is misrecognized for what it is. Ideology, though totalizing and often abstract in its effects, is not itself ungrounded. Language defines and constitutes particular ideologies in the reciprocal ways that ideologies guide and motivate the realization of linguistic choices. The interplay of language and ideology may then be metaphorized as the double chromosomal helix, two separate strands that are nevertheless intricately intertwined, neither of which is ever for a brief moment far from the other. Research on ideology must ground ideology solidly on a linguistic and social basis of individual and institutional constructions. Ideology is only abstract to the extent that for it to work, its effects are felt and lived, but not easily located or identified. Though pervasive and totalizing, a sound and methodological linguistic deconstruction of the discourse surrounding us will lead to heightened ideological awareness.

This work has gained tremendously from the central ideas borrowed from semiotics. By viewing law as a resource and a semiotic web of signs, we reinforce the idea of motivated signs and the mutual impingement of choices of particular significations on one another, as well as the indexicality of sign networks. Using the semiotic framework to talk about the judicial choices made in particular contexts has made more explicit the talk about signs and their realizations, thus lifting these discussions away from a network of potential resources to ground them in concrete examples of an actualized web of choices in the discourse.

In the interest of accuracy, an ethnographic view of the law must be one of the ways in which we conceptualize law. The ethnographic orientation of research in anthropology with its emphasis on sociolinguistic resources, discourse, speech acts, participant observation, linguistic and social interactions and their interrelations in the context of a political economy (Sherzer 1977) brings together under one rubric the linguistic, the social, and the linguistic-social. My work is built up in part from such an ethnographic commitment.

Sherzer pointed out that a common criticism directed at the ethnography of speaking is the tradition's preoccupation and "fascination with ritual, ceremonial, verbally artistic, and other marked and special uses of speech" (1977:50) and its corresponding failure to pay equal attention to 'ordinary' speech forms. In my view, the idea of 'ordinary' speech or language is problematic, and the indeterminate nature of the language of the judiciary (is it ordinary or ceremonial, or both?) certainly causes problems for the distinction between the ceremonial and the ordinary. Judicial discourse lies somewhere between the ceremonial/ritualistic and the ordinary. It is ceremonial and ritualistic with respect to its legal functions to establish rulings and to interpret the law. It is ordinary because it is a discourse that draws from daily discourses and, though ritualistic and highly specialized, judicial language remains a part of the social fabric as it inscribes the regularities of daily decorum. In this unique form of discourse, the ceremonial aspects of language use in the institutional ceremony of a high Court situated in the context of the society and culture, and in the performance of judicial duties in a present-day context, merges with the regulated ordinariness that pervades life in American society. In many ways then, the language of judges is an 'ordinary' language which the layperson could access, though it certainly requires effort, but it is nevertheless a language that is also dressed with the power of institutional ceremony and rituals and is for this reason not wholly accessible to the general public.

Apart from Bauman's work on the seventeenth-century Quakers (1983), there has been little ethnographic work done on historical forms of discourse. Unlike Bauman's work, however, there are at least two potentially problematic issues that I have to deal with in relation to my use of historical texts.

First, much of the work that has been done in the ethnographic framework deals primarily with ways of speaking. The type of judicial discourse that I have studied here has been argued to be an instance of highly planned discourse that I call a kind of talk-text due to both its orality and its written-ness. I suggest here that the judicial opinion as a kind of talk-text serves to bridge the ethnographic focus on speech and to extend the ethnographic concern to the realm of the written word. Judicial discourse thus simultaneously illustrates the power of both the spoken *and* the written word, and more importantly, the language of judges constitutes the "cultural focus" that Bauman talks about (1983: 10). As Bauman says, "[i]f we consider that a cultural focus is a cultural domain in which meanings, forms, and values are especially heavily elaborated, we may expect to find in such spheres some of the richest and most powerful symbols of a given culture" (p.10). And indeed this is precisely the reason why I focus on judicial discourse – it is, in my view, one of the most important loci of cultural meanings and a powerfully symbolic and an organizing principle of American life.

Second, I do not work with the advantage of historical records that are at Bauman's disposal. In fact, the only type of judicial discourse that is made public is the published opinion in each case. The oral exchanges in the Supreme Court are not readily available either in terms of recordings or transcription.[5] The briefs, court memos, notes taken at judicial meetings in private chambers, earlier drafts of judicial opinions and so on are all unavailable for consultation. In fact, a recent donation of the late Justice Thurgood Marshall's papers to the Library of Congress created a major controversy among members of the Court, the main reasons for their protest being that making private judicial papers available to the public may cause embarrassment to existing justices and can possibly adversely affect the power and mystique of the Court (Greenhouse 1993). In addition to this, apart from the confirmation process by the Senate, Supreme Court justices rarely grant interviews to the press, and much of the justices' lives are shrouded behind a heavy veil of mystery.[6] The recent public lecture given by Justice Antonin Scalia at Princeton University is considered a rare occurrence (Greenhouse 1995a).

Given the general inaccessibility of judges and their private discourses, the characterization of judicial discourse within an ethnographic framework is made more problematic. I do not have the luxury of participant observation,[7] or any kind of records that will help me to fully contextualize my data. There is, however, the possibility of accessing secondary sources for information, such as interviews with former law clerks and lawyers involved in particular cases, if these are relatively recent.[8] While direct access to the court culture is limited to some extent, it is more important to emphasize that the general inaccessibility of the court to the public constitutes a defining feature of the judicial culture. A central part of doing ethnography about the high court and its judges is that the information that one gets is not direct, and is not gained through participant observation *per se*, but is instead gotten through indirect means, such as from judicial writings and the occasional expressed view of the judges themselves that get reported in the media. Information from the Court about the Court itself is thus filtered down to the observer and is not something that is there for the asking. In short, instead of viewing this as a problem, though I will certainly acknowledge the limitation on research imposed by the restrictions, I prefer to view the restrictions as part and parcel of studying the precise nature of this particular court culture. And for this reason, it really makes little significant difference whether the discourse I study is as removed as 1872 or as recent as 1973 since the restrictions imposed by the Court is such that even the most recent context is at best a remote or distant context. In fact, the limitation I am speaking of here poses an interesting challenge to those interested in studying the courts or similar types of closed cultures or communities. The challenge is: how do we make full use of what little we have in order to arrive at a reasonable characterization of the culture under study? Since the available information is restricted, I argue that this is yet one more reason for crossing disciplinary borders so that what may be lost through viewing things one way may be recovered and enriched by using another perspective.

There is, however, a potential complication involved in adopting a multidisciplinary approach to research. I call this the 'problem' of eclecticism. Multidisciplinarity enables me to view the nature of judicial discourse from different angles and at different levels of analysis, thus locating my work at the crossroads of many disciplines. This is an important advantage because such an approach underscores the complexities of the issues involved and it is truer to an ethnographic understanding of society and culture. I am, however, aware that there exist strong resistances to eclecticism, because there may be objections that an eclectic approach borrows too much from too many sources. Borrowing from too many sources is not in itself a problem; what is important is that what is borrowed must be useful to the task at hand. What may be problematic is the possibility of internal contradictions between these frameworks. Accompanying every framework is a set of terms and ideas as well as the peculiar meanings attached to these terms and ideas. When multiple frameworks are used within one context, these different sets of terms and ideas may actually conflict with one another. I do not think that there is much that we can do to avoid this problem except to be critical when transporting ideas into new contexts and to try and resolve the contradictions whenever we become aware of them.

4. A question of ethnographic standing: From the 'non-native' point of view

Is there value or validity in doing ethnography when the researcher is not a member of the community being studied? Much of received scholarship has argued for the importance on the researcher's part to develop and cultivate a 'native' understanding of the culture being studied.[9] This belief in the superiority of the 'native' viewpoint over that of The Other, or the 'non-native,' is readily evident from the approach adopted by many prominent scholars in various fields, but particularly perhaps, in anthropology and sociolinguistics. Witness for example, the titles of works by Clifford Geertz (1983) "From the native's point of view" and Charles Briggs' (1986) *Learning How to Ask*. Geertz, for example, writes that the question of the 'native's' viewpoint is better conceived "in terms of how anthropological analysis is to be conducted and its results framed, rather than what psychic constitution anthropologists need to have", thus "reduc[ing] the mystery of what 'seeing things from the native's point of view' means" (1983: 57–58). Though Geertz's goal was to find a means to make explicit what 'natives' know about their own cultures, Geertz did not go far enough to problematize the notion of the 'native'. Reframing the problem does not quite solve it, in my view. In sociolinguistics too, scholars clamour to access the relevant codes that will give them access to foreign communities, and at the same time, constantly try to develop better ways of participating and observing the targeted culture.

The debates surrounding the native-non-native issue continue to be difficult to resolve.[10] Whether one holds that the natives know too much and are not objective enough or non-natives don't understand otherness and often engage in ethnocentric thinking, the problem remains that objectivity is difficult to operationalize and ethnocentricism, while deplorable for many, is not easy to circumvent, given our situatedness. But such difficulties should not be taken to mean that these issues can be ignored.

When I first undertook this research in the earlier part of the 1990s, I was a graduate student pursuing my doctoral degree in linguistics at the University of Texas at Austin. As a Singaporean non-law student, I found myself an outsider in more ways than one. In a nutshell, I am a 'non-native' researcher, exploring issues that are *not* a 'natural' part of my own life experiences.

In law, there is an important notion known as "standing". Legal standing may be viewed in two ways. First, 'standing' is defined as "a position from which one may validly make a legal claim or seek to enforce a right or duty"; and second, "[o]ne is said to have *standing* when one's arguments on the merits of a case are able to be heard by an adjudicator" (Garner 1987:515). In other words, a person is said to have "standing" if he/she can show that his/her claim is a valid one, and this validity must be one that is accepted and recognized by the court. I appropriate this notion of legal standing and apply it to the issue at hand. My question is: does a 'non-native' researcher like me have what I will term "ethnographic standing"? In other words, are my 'non-native' observations valid and will the value of 'non-native' scholarship be recognized?

The question of who is or is not a 'native' in a community is a difficult one. I am inclined to believe that the search for the 'native' or 'native's viewpoint' is the result of the exoticization of Otherness that has then evolved into a kind of an ethnographic fiction. As in any discipline, sociolinguistics and anthropology are no different in their perceived need to legitimize their object of study and their methods of conducting research. One has only to recall the several attempts by prominent linguists to establish the scientific nature of linguistic research (the 'linguistics as a science'-type articles) for example, to see the legitimation process at work. The importance of studying another culture other than one's own, the emphasis placed on the value of field work and on the direct contact with the culture to be studied – these points are often impressed on students in these disciplines, perhaps more so in anthropology.

It has always struck me as ironical that in the call for the 'native's' point of view, researchers choose actually to go out of their way (literally) in pursuit not of their own communities but of an alien culture. Once the Other is identified, researchers then devote much time and energy to developing non-intrusive techniques to integrate into the community (hence the perpetual concern and anxieties over the "Observer's paradox"), the aim being to experience and understand the life of the Other *as if* it is one's own. The ethnographic descriptions that result are then touted as being a view from 'the inside', that is, from the 'native's' point of view! I am not trying to downgrade the authenticity of such efforts; I have every admiration for the dedication of individuals who commit themselves to developing such cross-cultural understandings. Apart from my personal anxieties about problems of representation and the risk of ethnocentric bias, what I am also questioning here is: isn't there a better way of doing research and are our energies not better channelled into more efficient ways of conceptualizing our scholarship?

In my opinion, if we want to access the 'native's' viewpoint, we should do the kind of research that has been labelled "homework". This is not to say that we should stop studying other cultures, or that we should stop trying to develop a sound understanding of what we choose to do. What I am rejecting here is not the sociolinguistic and anthropological pursuit of understanding foreign cultures, but I share the view of scholars who also question the exclusive need for the 'native's' viewpoint. In short, the 'native's' viewpoint needs to undergo a critical re-examination: If we accept that the obsession with the 'native' and the 'native's viewpoint' is a misguided tendency in our discipline, then we should restore the 'non-native' to his/her rightful position, thus in effect recognizing the value, validity, or ethnographic 'standing' of the 'non-native' researcher. In fact, we should exploit what a 'non-native' viewpoint can inform us about ourselves, about Otherness, and about the existing plurality of worldviews.

Putting the troublesome debates of who is the real 'native' aside, the value that I see in ethnography conducted from the 'non-native' point of view is that the outsider tends not to treat 'native' categories as natural in the way that 'natives' socialized into the culture are likely to do. Hence, the 'non-native' has the privilege of distance and as a result, this *dis*interested (not *un*interested) stance can actually be more critical and discerning than the view could possibly be from 'the inside'. Hence, my privileged position as 'an outsider' looking 'into' American law and society is a valuable asset. I am however keenly aware of the problems associated with the claim to objectivity and distance of the outsider. For me, objectivity is a relative matter. Being a disinterested observer, I find myself running less risk of romanticizing the culture I studied and in this sense, I am more 'objective' than a 'native' might be in the same situation. But I will concede that the value of 'native' knowledge lies in its implicit understanding (by virtue of membership) of the complexities of its own community and rules in ways that are not always clear to the outsider.

In representing the Other, one often discovers one's own self. In the discovery of the self through studying the Other, I argue that one becomes even more equipped to comment on the Other. This is another reason why a 'non-native' point of view can be an advantage, for it is by way of contrast that the Other is revealed. This contrast is, of course, not a possibility with a 'native' researcher. In fact, one often hears of the difficulties 'natives' have in interrogating the self, due to the lack of distance. Under these circumstances, 'non-nativeness' is an asset, not a liability.

Finally, insofar as I can claim to have successfully accessed the terms of American society from the point of view of law, then I can claim some degree of validity and confidence in my ethnographic study of American (legal) culture. In short, ethnographic standing is not, in my view, the sole dominion of 'native' or 'near-native' researchers alone.

Given all that has been said above, the question of who is the 'native' in my context becomes understandably problematic. Or, what does being 'native' mean? Are the Americans I encountered more or less 'native' than me, the alien researcher who has become an informed outsider and who has to some extent tapped into the temper of American culture? There is obviously no easy answer here, and personally, I believe that this is no longer a relevant or interesting question to start with. It is, however, crystal clear to me that skin colour, birthrights, and citizenship have little to do with 'nativeness'. While having access to a community's language, beliefs, values, lifestyles, laws and ideology are all undeniably beneficial to one who seeks a deeper understanding of a culture, the 'non-native' viewpoint is unequivocally not without its merits. In fact, when carefully exploited, the naïvete´ of a 'non-native' can inform in ways that the socialized, enculturated 'native' may not be able to achieve. Seen in this light, *the knowledge gained from the view from the 'outside' can valuably supplement and complement the view from the 'inside'.* In such a combined effort of both kinds of knowledge, a better characterization of particular cultures may be achieved.

One final but necessary qualification should be included here. Over and above the 'native' or 'non-native' perspective, it is important to acknowledge that my viewpoint is by its very nature a necessarily ideological one. I would be making a mockery of my own study of the linguistic and social constructions of ideology and worldviews if I even hint at the 'objectivity' of my own viewpoint. As Mannheim (1936) argued decades ago, the conception of ideology has to be total, general, and non-evaluative. I draw particular attention to Mannheim's stress on the *general* (as opposed to the special) conception of ideology. Mannheim wrote that (p.61):

> As long as one does not call his [or her] own position into question but regards it as absolute, while interpreting his [or her] opponents' ideas as a mere function of the social positions they occupy, the decisive step forward has not yet been taken. . In contrast to [the] special formulation, the general form of the total conception of ideology is being used by the analyst when he [or she] has the courage to subject not just the adversary's point of view but all points of view, including his [or her] own, to the ideological analysis.

My own viewpoint is thus to be qualified as constituting just such a perspective, laden with my own prejudices and my ideological commitments, and hence, is limited to what I can see, and perhaps, more importantly, by what I choose to see.

Unlike Labov's (1982) view that scientific objectivity and social commitment are potentially conflicting goals to be resolved in linguistic research, I share Keith Walters' view that objectivity, commitment and ideology intermesh with one another to yield a subjectivity that is inevitably personal and political (Walters 1995 SALSA keynote). In this light, the resolution of conflicts is not the issue here. Instead, the relevant issue is the question of a critical awareness of ideology permeating even our most noble commitments and our conscientious pursuit of objectivity. This is the reason for adopting a critical perspective – to impose on ourselves the required vigilance that will ensure that our efforts are as far removed from prejudice as we can possibly make them. For those who think that I am laying myself open to criticisms by admitting my own ideological viewpoint, I repeat the wisdom that Pratt (1982:154) has eloquently expressed:

> Some may wish to argue that such commitments have no place in academic investigations, or in linguistics, but I think they are wrong. To begin with, that argument is obviously as ideologically committed as my own. More generally, any discourse has ideological dimensions – values – just as it has esthetic and sociological ones. Poetics and sociolinguistics are equipping us with a stylistics that can deal with these latter two dimensions. Ultimately, we will need a stylistics that can deal with the first one too.

Finally, I choose (a last act of ideological posturing!) to let Virginia Woolf have the last words on the subjectivity of 'truth' (1929:4):

> At any rate, when a subject is highly controversial. .one cannot hope to tell the truth. One can only show how one came to hold whatever opinion one does hold. One can only give one's audience the chance of drawing their own conclusions as they observe the limitations, the prejudices, the idiosyncracies of the speaker.

5. Where do we go from here? New challenges for a new millennium

According to Baer (1999:16–17),

> Feminist jurisprudence has made creative use of theories of gendered reality and seeks to provide explicit female orientation to counter implicit male orientation.

If feminist jurisprudence has indeed made such progress, then what else remains to be done as we move into the future? Or put differently, given what we now know about how courts operate with respect to women's issues, what should feminist jurisprudence aim to do? In other words, what are the issues that still need to be addressed, and what are the agendas that feminists still need to push for in the years to come?

As Buker (1999:3) has argued, feminist scholars, especially those working within feminist jurisprudence, are particularly "well-positioned to contribute to American politics because the law provides a key discourse for talking about justice". More specifically,

> Feminist jurisprudence connects public life and the law by focusing on issues of gender. Thus, it can help citizens develop new ways of understanding justice that enables the courts to serve female and male citizens more fairly (1999:3–4).

And indeed much feminist effort over the decades has gone into doing just this.

Contemporary feminist efforts have devoted energies to issues of empowerment – to give power to those who lack power, through education and consciousness-raising activities. Yet, despite these extensive efforts, as Catharine MacKinnon wrote in her paper, "Reflections on law in everyday life of women" (1993: 109–110):

> Most women will tell you that law has little to do with their everyday lives. They seldom hit walls that look legal – they do not get that far. The lives of women in poverty are circumscribed by rules and regulations that they know are stacked and enforced against them and could be different, but nothing so majestic as "the law" is accessible to them. Many women encounter official obstacles, but few have the law in their hands.... To most women, the law is a foreign country with an unintelligible tongue, alien mores, secret traps, uncontrollable and unresponsive dynamics, obscure but rigid dogmas, barbaric and draconian rituals, and consequences as scary as they are incomprehensible.... Most women feel that the law is not about them, has no idea who they are or what they face or how they think or feel, has nothing to say to them, and can do nothing for them. When the law and their life collide, it is their life that gets the worst of it.

It is indeed tragic that an institution that bears so directly on people's lives has been experienced to be such a "foreign country" with "alien mores". Despite all the work that has been done in the last two decades, it seems that for many people, law remains an impenetrable and negative experience. In this light, I believe that what remains as part of the future challenge for feminist jurisprudence is to ensure that this foreign-ness is alleviated so that law becomes more comprehensible to the ordinary person in the street, and more of an ally in people's everyday lives.

If women (and men) only know what their rights are and how the law can be used as a forum to fight for and maintain those rights, I believe we can work towards a time when an encounter with the law need not be so terrifying that it leaves us with a feeling of less power than we started out. However, as MacKinnon cautions, law and power are not similarly experienced by women in the way they are experienced by men (p.119), simply because the history of our experiences with both law and power differ. Hence, MacKinnon maintains that "[w]omen need institutional support for equality, both because of and in spite of the fact that power in women's hands is different from power in men's hands" (p.121). This is where feminist jurisprudence can play a crucial role – feminist scholars can act as brokers who help bridge the gap between the laypersons and the institution. As a voice in society, and an increasingly powerful one with substantial amount of influence, I believe that feminist scholars are uniquely positioned both in terms of their knowledge about law and the nature of institutions and in terms of their sympathy for those less privileged to facilitate the necessary connections. Unless this bridge is built, for a large part, law will remain an alienating experience for many.

The alienation that is felt by the average person with regard to the legal institution is also shared by women who work within the legal institution itself. As Baer (1999: 71), among others, has noted,

> Women who come to law and jurisprudence work within a male tradition. Law has been a male activity. It is now a male activity in which both men and women engage.

This status quo is, of course, a very unfortunate and unsatisfactory state of affairs. Even though it is suggested above that though law remains a male institution, it is, at minimum, now a male institution that *includes* women. Women's entry into the legal profession as viable contributors is indeed progress given our history of exclusion, but the value of such inclusiveness is vastly limited if women are forced to adopt a male style and to work within a mould not of their own making. Like the woman in the street, this kind of access is limited in scope as the law remains for even these professional women, a foreign land. Hence, feminist scholars and women lawyers have to take up this challenge: to transform the law and the institution in ways that can be said to truly accommodate and include women in real terms.

The other important role that feminist scholars can continue to play is to make use of the legal forum to urge the courts to pay more attention to gender issues in general, and to steer the courts towards more heightened awareness with regard to women's issues in particular. As an institutional voice itself (i.e. academic), feminist (legal) scholars are well situated to speak on behalf of those whose voices are muted. Though the courts have come a long way since the *Bradwell* era in their treatment of gender, I believe there is still much room for even more enlightened decisions. The institutional support that women need to obtain equality in society is not just something that must be a priority on feminist agendas, but must also come from the (legal) institution itself. After all, of all social institutions, does law not have a higher stake than any other institution in ensuring equality and rights protection for the citizenry?

One useful contribution that feminist scholars can make is to help to bring about change with respect to the court's appeal to precedents in constructing judicial arguments. Buker (1999: 50) puts it best when she says that because law originates and developed from a male-centred perspective,

> precedent is hopelessly mired in patriarchy. However, a feminist hermeneutic can reread some of these earlier precedents and offer alternative constructions of male-female relationships.

Buker illustrates this viewpoint by noting the result in *Roe v. Wade* for example, where years of feminist efforts have helped to shift the responsibility for the abortion decision away from the state and gave it to women, at least in the first trimester (Buker 1999: 51). By laying the groundwork for a re-reading and reconstruction of gender roles, feminist scholars have in this way contributed positively in helping to reshape the direction of the law.

Apart from meeting this challenge to facilitate much needed connections between laypersons and institutions, I believe that the other major challenge for feminist practices is to engage in a critical, self-reflexive examination of its own practices. Just as "justice is made by people who live in a world already made", the theories and the practices of (mainstream) feminist jurisprudence are also wrapped in the ideologies of the mainstream white feminist culture and its particular modes of thinking. In other words, while feminist jurisprudence offers us a valuable point of view for re-examining law and legal culture, its theories are themselves also tied to a particular dominant culture. Baer (1999: 31) characterized this problem in the following way:

> Just as conventional theory has excluded women, feminist theory has excluded minority women. As "majority" feminist scholars accuse conventional theory of male bias, they find themselves accused by minority feminists of white, middle-class, and heterosexual bias. Explicit specificity in feminist theory has privileged some viewpoints and excluded others as much as the implicit specificity of conventional theory has.

This problem posed from the perspective of minority scholars including myself, an Asian feminist, is well-known by now – even though women all over share certain basic predicaments, the fact is women are NOT the same in any one place; the category 'woman' sweeps across all types of diversities crosscut by class, economic status, education, cultural practices and so on. So, the theories and practices of (white, mainstream) feminist jurisprudence cannot apply to all in the same way.

Patricia Cain (1990) notes that "current feminist legal theory is deficient and impoverished because it has not paid sufficient attention to the real life experiences of women who do not speak the 'dominant discourse'". Even when it proclaims to listen to women's voices in addressing the issues, it nevertheless translates or is forced to translate diverse women's voices into one language – the dominant one. Just as feminists have worried over the translation of female voices by male ones, this translation of minority women's voices by mainstream feminist ones should also be a cause for worry.

Mainstream/dominant feminist paradigms must be made more conscious of their own hegemonic practices and assumptions. They must be more self-reflexive and must be willing to be critical of themselves. Such vigilance must be upheld or such practices will just be yet another domineering, oppressive paradigm, oppressing lesser candidates when their aims are to promote equal treatment and fairness. Dominant paradigms must therefore find a way to avoid exclusion of otherness. I am not certain if this is theoretically possible – after all, all forms of theorizing are ideological. But there must at least be an understanding of such a possibility of exclusion; and genuine attempts must be made towards more inclusive formulations. Awareness must therefore be built into the (dominant) theorizing and practices. Whatever we do, we must avoid excluding other women when we were once ourselves unfortunate enough to experience the bitter taste of exclusion. This is indeed a challenge we must meet and a promise that we must strive to keep in the years ahead.

Notes

Chapter 1

1. John B. Carroll first introduced the term "Sapir-Whorf Hypothesis" in his introduction to an anthology of Whorf's work (1956:27). Hill and Mannheim (1992:386) have since drawn attention to the problems of the label "hypothesis". They argue that "the linguistic relativity of Boas, Sapir, and Whorf is an axiom.... As with other working assumptions, ... it can only be judged on the basis of the extent to which it leads to productive questions about talk and social action, not by canons of falsifiability".

2. This is a term that is coined by Milroy and Milroy (1985).

3. For an anthology of legal narratives in general, I refer interested readers to a collection edited by David Ray Papke (1991). The use and the importance of narrative have also been underscored by scholars such as Robin West (1993) and Eloise Buker (1999), among others.

Chapter 2

1. As James Clifford said in his work on the Mashpee trial, he can only limit himself to "the reality of a specific interest and field of vision" (1988:290); the same goes for my work here.

2. Benson's use of the semiotic web comes from Sebeok (1975), which may be traced as far back as Holmes' (1897) idea of the law as a seamless web.

3. For an alternative view of the law, see Barron (2000), where she insists that law is "not literature, or art, or poetry, or even primarily a 'system of meaning'" but is most crucially "a system of *prescriptions*" (pp.278–279).

4. For a provocative discussion of issues of interpretation and literal meaning, please see *A Matter of Interpretation: Federal Courts and the Law* by Antonin Scalia, Princeton University Press, N.J., 1997.

Chapter 3

1. The *Bradwell* case is sometimes dated as 1873, but here, I follow the 1872 date given by the United States Report, Volume 83, where I obtained the *Bradwell* text.

2. In my view, the disagreement between the Court's characterization of the problem as involving marriage and Myra's own characterization as gender is not a real conflict of interpretation. Since men, married or single, do not face the same problem as women,

married or single, in the *Bradwell* era, I feel that it is the combination of both gender and marriage that was seen as problematic by the Court.

3. See *Blackstone Commentaries*, reproduced in the Appendix.

4. Henceforth, unless otherwise indicated, italics placed in the numbered examples are mine.

5. More discussion of the use of the word "person" will be offered in a later section on semantic shifts.

6. I hasten to note that the very idea of "generic usage" inscribes a bias towards one gender, even when it professes to be inclusive in meaning.

7. It is interesting to note that, on the one hand, woman is relegated to the *private* world of the home, but on the other hand, her health is said to be a matter of *public* concern. This contradiction, like the argument for restricting work hours *outside* but not *within* the home, is not surprising as the Court foregrounds certain arguments and not others.

8. Verbs of 'saying', 'material' and 'relational' verbs are all concepts that I adopt from Halliday (1985). Briefly, verbs of 'saying' are verbs which denote speech; material verbs describe some kind of (physical) action; and relational verbs denote relationships of identity, possession and attribution.

9. The verb in (16) is in the past tense and may thus be viewed as not strictly performative in nature. However, I argue that the acts expressed by such verbs are performative speech acts in the original context.

10. Examples of adjacency pairs include question-answer, invitation-acceptance, greeting-response,' etc.

11. An example of an old form cited in Sweetser's work is the Old English form "magan" which means "be strong, be able".

12. The *Slaughterhouse Cases* (1872) involved a constitutional challenge brought by a group of butchers against the Louisiana legislation that created a private monopoly of the slaughterhouse trade, thus prohibiting parties other than the state-sanctioned corporation to operate slaughterhouses.

13. In this case, armed service regulations dictated that only the spouses of male service personnel qualify as dependents for the purpose of collecting medical and dental benefits, and not vice versa. The court's 8–1 decision finally struck down the regulations.

14. A Rhode Island statute disallowed class C liquor licensees who operate bars on premises where no food is prepared from serving women on the grounds that such places are especially dangerous for women.

15. *Lochner* involved a statute that restricted a person's right to work in a bakery for more than sixty hours a week or ten hours a day. The court ruled that this restriction is invalid, as it infringes on a man's (but not a woman's) right to freedom of contract.

16. By statute, women are prohibited from working in restaurants in large cities between the hours of ten in the evening and six in the morning, due to the "the dangers and menaces incident to night life in large cities".

17. An inmate seeks relief from the Court over an infringement of his rights over hair length regulations (not applicable to female inmates) and the required supervision over showers for homosexuals. The Court denied relief.

Chapter 4

1. I refer readers to a recent issue from the Supreme Court Historical Society, *Supreme Court Decisions and Women's Rights* (2001) for discussion of such cases.

Chapter 5

1. The comments here are not meant to reduce the issues in *Roe* to one involving only women's rights. I am aware that the abortion issue involves several important issues that pertain to women, men, and potential life, but here I restrict myself to issues that I see as most pertinent to my present concerns.

2. By some interpretations, *Reed* only goes so far as to question the unreasonableness of the Idaho statute that was involved, and hence the ruling, it has been noted, did not in fact go far enough to make gender a suspect classification.

3. Whether "equal treatment" means to be treated "the same" or "equitably" is a thorny issue that is at the centre of much contemporary legal debates. My point is that the Court seems to have moved away from an overtly preferential treatment of the male towards a position in which gender is either judged as irrelevant to the issue at hand, or as not the sole consideration in law.

4. As noted above, the abortion issue involves more than just women and men, but also covers issues involving foetal rights and potential life. It is precisely because the abortion issue has been cast in terms of competing rights, with certain groups foregrounding the right of the woman and other groups stressing the right of the foetus that makes the issue so ideologically charged.

5. With the following important exception: the Warren Court granted permission for tapings during several sessions beginning from 1955, and as a result, oral arguments for over 5000 cases presented to the United States Supreme Court are now available from the National Archives. The existence of these tapes are, however, not widely known outside legal circles, and the procedures for obtaining these tapes are said to be costly and time consuming. Excerpted transcripts of the legal arguments are now also available in the form of a book edited by Irons and Guitton (1993), with an accompanying set of tapes.

6. However, I have recently come across the book, *8 Men and a Lady: Profiles of the Justices of the Supreme Court*, published by the National Press (1990), which gives a rare look behind this judicial facade. The book seems to concentrate more on the backgrounds of the justices than on their judicial performances.

7. Seats in the Supreme Court for public observers are highly restricted. Tourists visiting the Supreme Court during court sessions are limited to the viewing gallery where each group is ushered in and out in a matter of three minutes!

8. My situation as a non-law graduate student in Texas has limited my access a great deal. However, as part of my research into *Roe v. Wade*, with thanks to Prof. Sarah Weddington, one of the attorneys in the case, I attended a class taught by her in Spring 1994, where the case was discussed. Apart from her class discussions, I have also read Weddington's (1992) account of the circumstances that led up to the case, and the reactions to it. In addition, I have also read Norma McCorvey's (she was Jane Roe) perspective on the case. Additional material on *Roe* is also available in Irons and Guitton (1993). As for *Bradwell v. Illinois*, I have found a book written by Jane Friedman (1993) to be invaluable in providing the background and the life story of Myra Bradwell, especially with Friedman's inclusion of Bradwell's own writings about her legal struggles.

9. The quotation marks placed on the terms 'native' and 'non-native' signal the problematic nature of these labels.

10. Several recent papers have continued to problematize the distinction between 'native' and 'non-native'. Examples include Hong (1994) and Narayan (1993).

Bibliography

Abraham, Kenneth S. 1981. "Three fallacies of interpretation: A comment on precedent and judicial decision". *23 Arizona Law Review 771.*

Abrams, Kathryn. 1994. "The narrative and the normative in legal scholarship". In *Representing Women: Law, Literature, and Feminism,* Susan Sage Heinzelman and Zipporah Batshaw Wiseman (eds), 44–56. Durham and London: Duke University Press.

Anderson, Benedict. 1983. *Imagined Communities: Reflections on the Origin and Spread of Nationalism.* London: verso.

Austin, J.L. 1962. *How to do Things with Words.* New York: Oxford University Press.

Baer, Judith A. 1999. *Our Lives Before the Law: Constructing a Feminist Jurisprudence,* New Jersey: Princeton University Press.

Bakhtin, Mikhail M. 1929/1973. *Problems of Dostoevsky's Poetics.* Ann Arbor, MI: Ardis.

Barron, Anne. 2000. "Feminism, aestheticism and the limits of law". *Feminist Legal Studies* 8:275–317.

Bartlett, Katharine T. and Kennedy, Rosanne . 1991 (eds). *Feminist Legal Theory: Readings in Law and Gender.* Boulder, Colo.: Westview Press, Inc.

Bartlett, Katharine T. and Kennedy, Rosanne. 1991. "Introduction". In *Feminist Legal Theory: Readings in Law and Gender,* Katharine T. Bartlett and Rosanne Kennedy (eds), 1–11. Boulder, Colo.: Westview Press.

Bauman, Richard. 1983. *Let Your Words Be Few: Symbolism of Speaking and Silence Among Seventeenth-Century Quakers.* Cambridge: Cambridge University Press.

Belo, Jane. 1970. "The Balinese temper". In *Traditional Balinese Culture.* Jane Belo (ed), 85–110. New York

Benson, James D., Cummings, Michael J., and Greaves, William S. 1988 (eds). *Linguistics in a Systemic Perspective.* Philadelphia: John Benjamins.

Benson, Robert W. 1988. "How judges fool themselves: The semiotics of the easy case". In *Law and Semiotics,* Vol. 2, Roberta Kevelson (ed), 31–60. New York: Plenum Press.

Blackstone, *William.* 1966. *Commentaries on the Laws of England,* Book1. Oceana.

Bobbitt, Philip. 1982. *Constitutional Fate: Theory of the Constitution.* New York: Oxford University Press.

Bobbitt, Philip. 1991. *Constitutional Interpretation.* Oxford: Basil Blackwell.

Bourdieu, Pierre. 1977/1991 "On symbolic power". In *Language and Symbolic Power,* Gino Raymond and Matthew Adamson (trs), John B. Thompson (ed), 163–170. Massachusetts: Harvard University Press.

Bourdieu, Pierre. 1982a/1991. "The production and reproduction of legitimate language". In *Language and Symbolic Power,* Gino Raymond and Matthew Adamson (trs), John B. Thompson (ed), 43–65. Massachusetts: Harvard University Press.

Bourdieu, Pierre. 1982b/1991. "Rites of institution". In *Language and Symbolic Power,* Gino Raymond and Matthew Adamson (trs), John B. Thompson (ed), 117–126. Massachusetts: Harvard University Press.

Bourdieu, Pierre. 1991. *Language and Symbolic Power.* Gino Raymond and Matthew Adamson (trs), John B. Thompson (ed). Massachusetts: Harvard University Press.

Briggs, Charles L. 1986. *Learning How To Ask: A Sociolinguistic Appraisal of the Role of the Interview in Social Science Research.* Cambridge: Cambridge University Press.

Buker, Eloise A. 1999. *Talking Feminist Politics: Conversations on Law, Science, and the Postmodern,* Lanham, Maryland: Rowman & Littlefield Publishers, Inc.

Butler, Judith. 1990. *Gender Trouble: Feminism and the Subversion of Identity.* New York: Routledge, Chapman and Hall, Inc.

Cain, Patricia A. 1990/1991. "Feminist jurisprudence: Grounding the theories". In *Feminist Legal Theory: Readings in Law and Gender,* Katharine T. Bartlett and Rosanne Kennedy (eds), 263–280. Boulder, Colo.: Westview Press.

Cameron, Deborah. 1990. "Demythologizing sociolinguistics: Why language does not reflect society". In *Ideologies of Language,* John E. Joseph and Talbot J.Taylor (eds), 79–93. London: Routledge and Kegan Paul.

Carroll, John B. 1956 (ed). "Introduction". In *Language, Thought, and Reality,* 1–34. Cambridge: MIT Press.

Cicourel, Aaron V. 1975. "Discourse and text: Cognitive and linguistic processes in studies of social structure". *Versus* 12:33–84.

Clifford, James. 1988. *The Predicament of Culture,* Cambridge: Harvard University Press.

Coates, Jennifer. 1983. *The Semantics of the Modal Auxiliaries.* London: Croom Helm.

Conley, John M. and O'Barr, William M. 1990. *Rules versus Relationships: The Ethnography of Legal Discourse.* Chicago: University of Chicago Press.

Coulthard, Malcolm and Montgomery, M. 1982. *Studies in Discourse Analysis.* London: Routledge and Kegan Paul.

Dalton, Clare. 1988. "An essay in the deconstruction of contract doctrine". In *Interpreting Law and Literature: A Hermeneutic Reader,* Sanford Levinson and Stephen Mailloux (eds), 285–318. Evanston: Northwestern University Press.

Delgado, Richard and Bell, Derrick. 1989. "Minority law professors' lives: The Bell-Delgado Survey". *24 Harvard Civ. Rts. Civ. Lib. Law Review 349.*

Drachman, Virginia G. 1998. *Sisters in Law: Women Lawyers in Modern American History,* Cambridge, Mass.: Harvard University Press.

Duranti, Alessandro. 1994. *From Grammar to Politics: Linguistic Anthropology in a Western Samoan Village.* Berkeley: University of California Press.

Duranti, Alessandro. 1997. *Linguistic Anthropology,* UK: Cambridge University Press.

Duranti, Alessandro and Goodwin, Charles. 1992 (eds) *Rethinking Context: Language as an Interactive Phenomenon.* New York: Cambridge University Press.

Dworkin, Ronald. 1982. "Law as interpretation". *60 Texas law Review 527.*

Evans, David T. 1993. *Sexual Citizenship: The Material Construction of Sexualities.* London: Routledge.

Fairclough, Norman. 1992. *Discourse and Social Change.* Cambridge: Polity Press.

Firth, John R. 1957. *Papers in Linguistics. 1934–1951.* London: Oxford University Press.

Fish, Stanley. 1989. "Working on the chain gang: Interpretation in law and literature". In *Doing What Comes Naturally: Change, Rhetoric, and the Practice of Theory in Literary and Legal Studies,* Stanley Fish, 87–102. Durham: Duke University Press.

Fishman, Joshua A. 1965. "Who speaks what language to whom and when?" *Linguistique* 2:67–88.

Foucault, Michel. 1972. *The Archaeology of Knowledge and the Discourse on Language.* A.M. Sheridan Smith (tr). U.K.: Tavistock Publications Ltd.

Foucault, Michel. 1972–1977/1980. *Power/Knowledge: Selected Interviews and Other Writings.* Colin Gordon (ed), Colin Gordon, Leo Marshall, John Mepham and Kate Soper (trs). New York: Harvester Press.

Foucault, Michel. 1978/1990. *The History of Sexuality. Volume 1: An Introduction.* Robert Hurley (tr). New York: Vintage Books.

Fowler, Roger . 1991. "Critical linguistics". In *The Linguistic Encyclopedia,* Kirsten Malmkjaer (ed), 89–93. London: Routledge and Kegan Paul.

Fowler, Roger, Hodge, Bob, Kress, Gunther, and Trew, Tony. 1979 *Language and Control.* London: Routledge and Kegan Paul.

Friedman, Jane M. 1993. *America's First Woman Lawyer: The Biography of Myra Bradwell.* New York: Prometheus Books.

Friedrich, Paul. 1989. "Language, ideology, and political economy". *American Anthropologist* 91:295–312.

Gal, Susan. 1989. "Language and political economy". *Annual Review of Anthropology. 18*:345–367.

Gal, Susan. 1991. "Between speech and silence: The problematics of research on language and gender". In *Gender at the Crossroads of Knowledge: Feminist Anthropology in the Postmodern Era,* Micaela di Leonardo (ed), Berkeley: University of California Press.

Gal, Susan. 1994. "Gender in the post-socialist transition: The abortion debate in Hungary". In *East European Politics and Societies* 8:256–286.

Garner, Bryan A. 1987. *A Dictionary of Modern Legal Usage.* Oxford: Oxford University Press.

Geertz, Clifford. 1973. "Deep play: Notes on the Balinese cockfight". In *The Interpretations of Cultures,* Clifford Geertz, 412–453. New York: Basic Books

Geertz, Clifford. 1983. ""From the native's point of view": On the nature of anthropological understanding. In *Local Knowledge: Further Essays in Interpretive Anthropology,* Clifford Geertz, 55–70. Basic Books.

Ginsburg, Ruth Bader. 1995. "Some thoughts on autonomy and equality in relation to *Roe v. Wade*". In *Feminist Legal Theory: Volume 1,* Frances E. Olsen (ed), 281–292. UK: Dartmouth Publishing Co. Ltd.

Greenhouse, Linda. 1993. "Justices' fear: Losing their mystique". *International Herald Tribune,* May 28, 1993.

Greenhouse, Linda. 1995a. "At the bar: Justice Scalia, cheerfully, tells what's behind following the letter of the law". *The New York Times,* March 17, 1995.

Greenhouse, Linda. 1995b. "In step on racial policy". *The New York Times,* June 14, 1995.

Halliday, Michael A.K. 1978. *Language as Social Semiotic: The Social Interpretation of Language and Meaning.* London: Edward Arnold.

Halliday, M.A.K. 1985/1994. *An Introduction to Functional Grammar.* Second Edition. London: Edward Arnold.

Halliday, M.A.K. 1989. *Spoken and Written Language*. Oxford: Oxford University Press.

Halliday, M.A.K. and Martin, J.R. 1981 (eds). *Readings in Systemic Linguistics*. London: Batsford.

Hill, Jane H. 1985. "The grammar of consciousness and the consciousness of grammar". *American Ethnologist* 12:725–737.

Hill, Jane H. and Mannheim, Bruce. 1992. "Language and world view". *Annual Review of Anthropology* 21:381–406.

Hodge, Bob and Kress, Gunther. 1979. *Language as Ideology*. London: Routledge and Kegan Paul.

Hodge, Bob and Kress, Gunther. 1988. *Social Semiotics*. U.K.: Polity Press.

Hoff, Joan. 1991. *Law, Gender, and Injustice: A Legal History of U.S. Women*. New York University Press.

Holmes, Oliver Wendell . 1897. "The path of the law". *10 Harvard Law Review 457.*

Hong, Kee Lung. 1994. "Experiences of being a "native" while observing anthropology". *Anthropology Today* 10:3:6–9.

Hymes, Dell. 1969/1974 (ed). *Reinventing Anthropology*. New York:vintage Books.

Hymes, Dell. 1972a. "Models of the interaction of language and social life". In *Directions in Sociolinguistics: The Ethnography of Communication*, John J. Gumperz and Dell Hymes (eds), 35–71 New York: Holt, Rinehart and Winston, Inc.

Hymes, Dell. 1972b. "The scope of sociolinguistics". In *Monograph Series on Languages and Linguistics: 23rd Annual Round Table. Sociolinguistics: Current Trends and Prospects*, Roger Shuy (ed), 313–333. Washington, D.C.: Georgetown University Press.

Hymes, Dell. 1973. "Speech and language: On the origins and foundations of inequality among speakers". *Daedalus* 102:59–85.

Hymes, Dell. 1974a. *Foundations in Sociolinguistics: An Ethnographic Approach*. Philadelphia: University of Pennsylvania Press.

Hymes, Dell. 1974b. "Ways of speaking". In *Explorations in the Ethnography of Speaking*, Richard Bauman and Joel Sherzer (eds), 433–451. London and New York: Cambridge University Press.

Irons, Peter and Guitton, Stephanie. 1993 (eds). *May It Please the Court: The Most Significant Oral Arguments Made Before the Supreme Court Since 1955*. New York: New Press.

Jakobson, Roman. 1990. "Langue and parole: Code and message". In *On Language*, Linda R. Waugh and Monique Monville-Burston (eds), 80–109. Cambridge, Mass.: Harvard University Press.

Joseph, John E. 1990. "Ideologizing Saussure: Bloomfield's and Chomsky's readings of the *Cours de linguistique generale*". In *Ideologies of Language*, John E. Joseph and Talbot J. Taylor (eds), 51–78. London: Routledge and Kegan Paul.

Kay, Herma Hill. 1988. *Sex-Based Discrimination: Text, Cases and Materials*. Third Edition. Minnesota: West Publishing Co.

Kay, Herma Hill. 1994. *Supplement to Sex-Based Discrimination: Text, Cases and Materials*. Third Edition. Minnesota: West Publishing Co.

Kevelson, Roberta. 1988. *The Law as a System of Signs.* New York: Plenum Press.

Kress, Gunther. 1989. *Linguistic Processes in Sociocultural Practice.* Oxford: Oxford University Press.

Kroch, A. and Small, C. 1978. "Grammatical ideology and its effects on speech". In *Linguistic Variation: Models and Methods,* David Sankoff (ed), 45–55. New York: Academic Press.

Labov, William. 1970. "The logic of nonstandard English". In *Georgetown University 20th Annual Round Table, Monograph Series on Languages and Linguistics,* James E. Alatis (ed), 1–43. Washington, D.C.: Georgetown University Press.

Labov, William. 1982. "Objectivity and commitment in linguistic science: The case of the Black English trial in Ann Arbor". *Language in Society* 11:165–201.

Lakoff, George and Johnson, Mark. 1980. *Metaphors We Live By.* Chicago: University of Chicago Press.

Lee, David. 1992. *Competing Discourses: Perspective and Ideology in Language.* New York: Longman.

Lindgren, J. Ralph and Taub, Nadine. 1988. *The Law of Sex Discrimination.* Minnesota: West Publishing Co.

Lippi-Green, Rosina. 1994. "Accent, standard language ideology, and discriminatory pretext in the courts". *Language in Society* 23:163–198.

Lippi-Green, Rosina. 1997. *English with an Accent: Language, Ideology, and Discrimination in the United States.* London and New York: Routledge.

MacKinnon, Catharine A. 1984/1991. "Difference and dominance: On sex discrimination". In *Feminist Legal Theory: Readings in Law and Gender,* Katharine T. Bartlett and Rosanne Kennedy (eds), 81–94. Boulder, Colo.: Westview Press, Inc.

MacKinnon, Catharine A. 1993. "Reflections on law in the everyday life of women". In *Law in Everyday Life,* Austin Sarat and Thomas R. Kearns (eds), 109–122. University of Michigan Press: Ann Arbor.

Mannheim, Karl. 1936/1994. "Ideology and utopia". In *Ideology,* Terry Eagleton (ed), 50–68. London and New York: Longman

Martin, J.R. 1989. *Factual Writing: Exploring and Challenging Social Reality.* U.K: Oxford University Press.

McCorvey, Norma. 1994. *I am Roe: My Life, Roe v. Wade, and Freedom of Choice.* New York: Harper Collins.

Menkel-Meadow, Carrie. 1987. "Excluded voices: New voices in the legal profession making new voices in the law". *42 University of Miami Law Review 29.*

Merry, S.E. 1986. "Everyday understandings of the law in working-class America". *American Ethnologist* 13:2:253–270.

Mills, C.W. 1940. "Situated actions and vocabularies of motive". *American Sociological Review* V:904–913. Reprinted in *Symbolic Interaction: A Reader in Social Psychology,* J.G. Manis and B.N. Meltzer (eds), 1967. Boston: Allyn and Bacon.

Milroy, James and Milroy, Lesley. 1985/1991. *Authority in Language: Investigating Language Prescription and Standardisation.* Second Edition. London: Routledge.

Minow, Martha. 1987. "Foreword: Justice engendered". *101 Harvard Law Review 10.*

Narayan, Kirin. 1993. "How native is a "native" anthropologist?" *American Anthropologist*, 95:3:671–686.

O'Barr, William M. and Atkins, Bowman K. 1980. "Women's language" or "Powerless language"? In *Women and Language in Literature and Society,* Sally McConnell-Ginet, Ruth Borker and Nelly Furman (eds), 93–110. New York: Praeger

Ochs, Elinor. 1992. "Indexing gender". In *Rethinking Context: Language as an Interactive Phenomenon,* Alessandro Duranti and Charles Goodwin (eds), 335–359. New York: Cambridge University Press.

Palmer, Frank R. 1986. *Mood and Modality.* Cambridge: Cambridge University Press.

Palmer, Frank R. 1990. *Modality and the English Modals.* Second Edition. London: Longman.

Papke, David Ray. 1991 (ed.). *Narrative and the Legal Discourse: A Reader in Storytelling and the Law.* Liverpool, U.K.: Deborah Charles Publications.

Peirce, Charles Sanders. 1931–1935. *Collected Papers,* 8 volumes. P. Weiss, C. Hartshorne and A. Burks (eds), 1958. Cambridge: Harvard University Press.

Pratt, Mary Louise . 1982. "Conventions of representation: Where discourse and ideology meet". In *Contemporary Perceptions of Language: Interdisciplinary Dimensions,* Heidi Byrnes (ed), 139–155. Washington, D.C.: Georgetown University Press.

Pratt, Mary Louise. 1987. "Linguistic utopias". In *The Linguistics of Writing: Arguments Between Language and Literature,* Nigel Fabb, Derek Attridge, Alan Durant and Colin MacCabe (eds), 48–66. Manchester: Manchester University Press.

Quine, W.V.O. 1961. *From a Logical Point of View.* New York: Harper and Row.

Saeed, John I. 1997. *Semantics.* Cambridge, Mass.: Blackwell Publishers.

Sapir, Edward. 1929/1966. "The status of linguistics as a science". In *Culture, Language and Personality: Selected Essays,* David G. Mandelbaum (ed), 65–77. Berkeley: University of California Press.

Sapir, Edward. 1933/1963. "Language". In *Selected Writings,* Edward Sapir, 7–32. Berkeley: University of California Press.

Scales, Ann C. 1986. "The emergence of feminist jurisprudence: An essay". *95 Yale Law Journal 1373.*

Scalia, Antonin. 1997. *A Matter of Interpretation: Federal Courts and the Law.* New Jersey: Princeton University Press.

Schultz, Vicki. 1992. "Women "before" the law: Judicial stories about women, work, and sex segregation on the job". In *Feminists Theorize the Political.* Judith Butler and Joan W. Scott (eds), 297–338. New York: Routledge, Chapman and Hall, Inc.

Searle, John. 1969 *Speech Acts.* Cambridge: Cambridge University Press.

Sebeok, Thomas A. 1975. "The semiotic web: A chronical of prejudices". *2 Bulletin of Literary Semiotics* 1–63.

Shepard's United States Citations: A Compilation of Citations to Decisions of the United States Supreme Court, 1994: volumes 1.1, 1.3, 1.7. Seventh Edition.

Sherzer, Joel. 1977. "The ethnography of speaking: A critical appraisal". In *Linguistics and Anthropology,* Muriel Saville-Troike (ed), 43–57. Washington, D.C.: Georgetown University Press.

Sherzer, Joel. 1983. *Kuna Ways of Speaking: An Ethnographic Perspective*. Austin: University of Texas Press.

Sherzer, Joel. 1987. "A discourse-centered approach to language and culture". *American Anthropologist* 89: 295–309.

Sherzer, Joel. 1989. "The Kuna verb: A study in the interplay of grammar, discourse, and style". In *General and Amerindian Ethnolinguistics*, M. Key and H. Hoenigswald (eds), 261–272. New York: Mouton de Gruyter.

Sherzer, Joel. 1990. *Verbal Art in San Blas: Kuna Culture Through its Discourse*. New York: Cambridge University Press.

Sherzer, Joel. 1993. "Review of David Lee, *Competing Discourses* (1992). *Language in Society* 22: 275–327.

Silverstein, Michael. 1979. "Language structure and linguistic ideology". In *The Elements: A Parasession on Linguistic Units and Levels*, P.R. Clyne, W.F. Hanks, and C.L. Hofbauer (eds), 193–247. Chicago: Chicago University Press.

Silverstein, Michael. 1985. "Language and the culture of gender: At the intersection of structure, usage, and ideology". In *Semiotic Mediation: Sociocultural and Psychological Perspectives*, Elizabeth Mertz and R. Parmentier (eds), 219–259. New York: Academic

Sinclair, John McH. and Coulthard, Malcolm. 1975. *Towards an Analysis of Discourse: The English Used by Teachers and Pupils*. Oxford: Oxford University Press.

Stanton, Elizabeth Cady, Anthony, Susan B. and Gage, Matilda Joslyn. 1861–1876/1881 (eds). *History of Woman Suffrage*, 3 volumes. New York: Fowler and Wells.

Sweetser, Eve. 1990. *From Etymology to Pragmatics: Metaphorical and Cultural Aspects of Semantic Structure*, New York: Cambridge University Press.

Tannen, Deborah. 1982a (ed). *Spoken and Written Language: Exploring Orality and Literacy*. Norwood, N.J.: Ablex.

Tannen, Deborah. 1982b (ed). *Coherence in Spoken and Written Discourse*. Norwood, N.J.: Ablex.

Tannen, Deborah. 1982c (ed). *Analyzing Discourse: Text and Talk*. Washington, D.C.: Georgetown University Press.

Taub, Nadine and Schneider, Elizabeth M. 1982. "Perspectives on women's subordination and the law". In *The Politics of Law: A Progressive Critique*, D. Kairys (ed), 117–139. New York: Pantheon.

Urban, Greg. 1991. *A Discourse-Centered Approach to Culture: Native South American Myths and Rituals*. Austin: University of Texas Press.

van Dijk, Teun A. 1998. *Ideology: A Multidisciplinary Approach*, London: Sage Publications.

Walters, Keith. 1995. "Contesting representations of African American language". Keynote presented at SALSA III, Austin, Texas, April 8, 1995.

Weddington, Sarah. 1992. *A Question of Choice*. New York: Penguin Books.

West, Robin. 1993. *Narrative, Authority, and Law*, Ann Arbor: University of Michigan Press.

Wexler, Natalie. 2001. "Sex discrimination: The search for a standard". In *Supreme Court Decisions and Women's Rights: Milestones to Equality*, Clare Cushman (ed), 37–67.

Washington, D.C.: CQ Press.

White, James Boyd. 1984. *When Words Lose Their Meaning: Constitutions and Reconstitutions of Language, Character, and Community.* Chicago: Chicago University Press.

White, James Boyd. 1985. *Heracles' Bow: Essays on the Rhetoric and Poetics of the Law.* Madison: University of Wisconsin Press.

White, James Boyd. 1988. "Judicial criticism". In *Interpreting Law and Literature: A Hermeneutic Reader,* Sanford Levinson and Stephen Mailloux (eds), 393–410. Evanston: Northwestern University Press.

Whorf, Benjamin Lee. 1941/1956. "The relation of habitual thought and behavior to language". In *Language, Thought, and Reality,* John B. Carroll (ed), 134–159. Cambridge: MIT Press.

Wittgenstein, Ludwig. 1922/1960. *Tractatus Logico-Philosophicus.* C. K. Ogden (tr). London: Routledge and Kegan Paul.

Wohl, Alexander. 2001. "Romantic paternalism: Barred from being lawyers". In *Supreme Court Decisions and Women's Rights: Milestones to Equality,* Clare Cushman (ed), 2–4. Washington, D.C.: CQ Press.

Woolf, Virginia. 1929. *A Room of One's Own.* New York: Harcourt Brace Jovanovich, Inc.

Worden, K.C. 1985. "Overshooting the target: A feminist deconstruction of legal education". *34 American University Law Review 1141.*

List of cases analyzed

Bradwell v. Illinois (1872), 83 U.S.(16 Wall.)130.
Muller v. Oregon (1908), 208 U.S.412.
Reed v. Reed (1971), 404 U.S. 71.
Roe v. Wade (1973), 410 U.S. 113.

List of cases cited

Batson v. Kentucky (1985), 476 U.S. 79
Brown v. Board of Education (1954), 347 U.S. 483.
Carey v. Population Services International (1977), 431 U.S. 678.
City of Akron v. Akron Center for Reproductive Health, Inc. (1983), 462 U.S. 416.
Doe v. Bolton (1973), 410 U.S. 179
Eisenstadt v. Baird (1972), 405 U.S. 438.
Faruki v. Rogers (1972), 349 F.S. 734.
Frontiero v. Richardson (1973), 411 U.S. 677.
Goesaert v. Cleary (1948), 335 U.S. 464.
Griswold v. Connecticut (1965), 381 U.S. 479.
Hoyt v. Florida (1961), 368 U.S. 57.
In re Lockwood (1894), 154 U.S. 116.
J.E.B. v. Alabama Ex Rel. T.B. (1994), 114 S.Ct.1419
Lochner v. New York (1905), 198 U.S. 45.
Minor v. Happersett (1874), 88 U.S. (21 Wall.)162.
Personal Administrator of Massachusetts v Feeney (1979), 442 U.S. 256.
Planned Parenthood of Central Missouri v. Danforth (1976), 428 U.S. 52.
Planned Parenthood of Southeastern Pennsylvania v. Casey (1992), 505 U.S.
Poe v. Werner (1974), 386 F.S. 1019.
Radice v. New York (1924), 264 U.S. 292.
Rosen v. Louisiana State Board of Medical Examiners (1974), 419 U.S. 1098.
Royster Guano Co. v. Virginia (1920), 253 U.S. 412.
Sail'er Inn, Inc. v. Kirby (1971), 485 P.2d 529.
Slaughterhouse Cases (1872), 83 U.S. (16 Wall.) 36.
Taylor v. Louisiana (1975), 419 U.S.522.
Union Pacific Railway Co. v. Botsford (1891), 141 U.S. 250.
Women's Liberation Union of Rhode Island v. Israel (1975), 512 F.2d. 109

Appendix I

Blackstone's Commentaries (1966), Book 1 Chapter 15

By marriage, the husband and wife are one person in law; that is, the very being or legal existence of the woman is suspended during the marriage, or at least is incorporated and consolidated into that of the husband, under whose wing, protection, and cover, she performs everything; and is, therefore, called in our law – French a *feme-covert, foemina viro co-operta*; is said to be *covert-baron*, or under the protection and influence of her husband, her *baron*, or lord; and her condition, during her marriage, is called coverture. Upon this principle, of an union of person in husband and wife, depend almost all the legal rights, duties, and disabilities, that either of them acquire by the marriage. I speak not at present of the rights of property, but of such as are merely personal. For this reason, a man cannot grant anything to his wife, or enter into covenant with her, for the grant would be to suppose her separate existence …

The husband also, (by the old law) might give his wife moderate correction; for, as he is to answer for her misbehavior, the law thought it reasonable to intrust him with this power of restraining her, by domestic chastisement, in the same moderation that a man is allowed to correct his apprentices or children; for whom the master or parent is also liable in some cases to answer …

These are the chief legal effects of marriage during the coverture; upon which we may observe, that even the disabilities which the wife lies under are, for the most part, intended for her protection and benefit. So great a favorite is the female sex of the laws of England!

Appendix II

Text 1: Bradwell v. Illinois, 83 U.S. (16 Wall.) 130 (1873)
Concurring opinion delivered by Justice Joseph Bradley

I concur in the judgment of the court in this case, by which the judgment of the Supreme Court of Illinois is affirmed, but not for the reasons specified in the opinion just read. The claim of the plaintiff, who is a married woman, to be admitted to practice as an attorney and counsellor-at-law, is based upon the supposed right of every person, man or woman, to engage in any lawful employment for a livelihood. The Supreme Court of Illinois denied the application on the ground that, by the common law, which is the basis of the laws of Illinois, only men were admitted to the bar, and the legislature had not made any change in this respect, but had simply provided that no person should be admitted to practice as attorney or counsellor without having previously obtained a license for that purpose from two justices of the Supreme Court, and that no person should receive a license without first obtaining a certificate from the court of some county of his good moral character. In other respects it was left to the discretion of the court to establish the rules by which admission to the profession should be determined. The court, however, regarded itself as bound by at least two limitations. One was that it should establish such terms of admission as would promote the proper administration of justice, and the other that it should not admit any persons, or class of persons, not intended by the legislature to be admitted, even though not expressly excluded by statute. In view of this latter limitation the court felt compelled to deny the application of females to be admitted as members of the bar. Being contrary to the rules of the common law and the usages of Westminster Hall from time immemorial, it could not be supposed that the legislature had intended to adopt any different rule. The claim that, under the fourteenth amendment of the Constitution, which declares that no State shall make or enforce any law which shall abridge the privileges and immunities of citizens of the United States, the statute law of Illinois, or the common law prevailing in that State, can no longer be set up as a barrier against the right of females to pursue any lawful employment for a livelihood (the practice of law included), assumes that it is one of the privileges and immunities of women as citizens to engage in any and every profession, occupation, or employment in civil life. It certainly cannot be affirmed, as an historical fact, that this has ever been established as one of the fundamental privileges and immunities of the sex. On the contrary, the civil law, as well as nature herself, has always recognized a wide difference in the respective spheres and destinies of man and woman. Man is, and should be, woman's protector and defender. The natural and proper timidity and delicacy which belongs to the female sex evidently unfits it for many of the occupations of civil life. The constitution of the family organization, which is founded in the divine ordinance, as well as in the nature of things, indicates the domestic sphere as that which properly belongs to the domain and functions of womanhood. The harmony, not to say identity, of interests and views which belong or should belong to the family institution, is repugnant to the idea of a woman adopting a distinct and independent career from that of her husband. So firmly fixed was this sentiment in the founders of the common law that it became a maxim of that system of jurisprudence that a woman had no legal existence separate from her husband, who was regarded as her head and representative in the social state; and, notwithstanding some recent modifications of this civil status, many of the special rules of law flowing from and dependent upon this cardinal principle still exist in full force in most States. One of these is, that a married woman is incapable, without her husband's consent, of making contracts which shall be binding on her or him.

This very incapacity was one circumstance which the Supreme Court of Illinois deemed important in rendering a married woman incompetent fully to perform the duties and trusts that belong to the office of any attorney or counsellor. It is true that many women are unmarried and not affected by any of the duties, complications, and incapacities arising out of the married state but these are exceptions to the general rule. The paramount destiny and mission of woman are to fulfill the noble and benign offices of wife and mother. This is the law of the Creator. And the rules of civil society must be adapted to the general constitution of things and cannot be based upon exceptional cases. The human movements of modern society, which have for their object the multiplication of avenues for woman's advancement, and of the occupation adapted to her condition and sex, have my heartiest concurrence. But I am not prepared to say that it is one of her fundamental rights and privileges to be admitted into every office and position, including those which require highly special qualifications and demanding special responsibilities. In the nature of things it is not every citizen of every age, sex, and condition that is qualified for every calling and position. It is the prerogative of the legislator to prescribe regulations founded on nature, reason, and experience for the due admission of skill and confidence. This fairly belongs to the police power of the State; and, in my opinion, in view of the peculiar characteristics, destiny, and mission of woman, it is within the province of the legislature to ordain what offices, positions, and callings shall be filled and discharged by men, and shall receive the benefit of those energies and responsibilities, and that decision and firmness which are presumed to predominate in the sterner sex. For these reasons I think that the laws of Illinois now complained of are not obnoxious to the charge of abridging any of the privileges and immunities of citizens of the United States.

Text 2: Muller v. Oregon, 208 U.S. 412 (1908)
Majority opinion of the court delivered by Justice Brewer (excerpt)

That woman's physical structure and the performance of maternal functions place her at a disadvantage in the struggle for subsistence is obvious. This is especially true when the burdens of motherhood are upon her. Even when they are not, by abundant testimony of the medical fraternity continuance for a long time on her feet at work, repeating this from day to day, tends to injurious effects upon the body, and as healthy mothers are essential to vigorous offspring, the physical well-being of woman becomes an object of public interest and care in order to preserve the strength and vigor of the race. Still again, history discloses the fact that woman has always been dependent upon man. He established his control at the outset by superior physical strength, and this control in various forms, with diminishing intensity, has continued to the present. As minors, though not to the same extent, she has been looked upon in the courts as needing especial care that her rights may be preserved. Education was long denied her, and while now the doors of the school room are opened and her opportunities for acquiring knowledge are great, yet even with that and the consequent increase of capacity for business affairs it is still true that in the struggle for subsistence she is not an equal competitor with her brother. Though limitations upon personal and contractual rights may be removed by legislation, there is that in her disposition and habits of life which will operate against a full assertion of those rights. She will still be where some legislation to protect her seems necessary to secure a real equality of right. Doubtless there are individual exceptions, and there are many respects in which she has an advantage over him; but looking at it from the viewpoint of the effort to maintain an independent position in matters from the other sex, she is properly placed in a class by herself, and legislation designed for her protection may be sustained, even when like legislation is not necessary for men and could not be sustained. It is impossible to close one's eyes to the fact that she still looks to her brother and depends upon him. Even though all restrictions on political, personal and contractual rights were taken away, and she stood, so far as statutes are concerned, upon an absolutely equal plane with him, it would still be true that she is so constituted that she will rest upon and look to him for protection; that her physical structure and a proper discharge of maternal functions – having in view not only her own health, but the well-being of the race – justify legislation to protect her from the greed as well as the passion of man. The limitations which this statute places upon her contractual powers, upon her right to agree with her employer as to the time she shall labor, are not imposed solely for her benefit, but also largely for the benefit of all. Many words cannot make this plainer. The two sexes differ in structure of body, in the functions to be performed by each, in the amount of physical strength, in the capacity for long-continued labor, particularly when done standing, the influence of vigorous health upon the future well-being of the race, the self-reliance which enables one to assert full rights, and in the capacity to maintain the struggle for subsistence. This difference justifies a difference in legislation and upholds that which is designed to compensate for some of the burdens which rest upon her.

For these reasons, and without questioning in any respect the decision in *Lochner v. New York*, we are of the opinion that it cannot be adjudged that the act in question is in conflict with the Federal Constitution, so far as it respects the work of a female in a laundry, and the judgment of the Supreme Court of Oregon is affirmed.

Text 3: Reed v. Reed, 404 U.S. 71 (1971)

Majority opinion of the Court delivered by Chief Justice Burger (excerpt)

Sally Reed ... appealed for review by this Court. and we noted probable jurisdiction. Having examined the record and considered the briefs and oral arguments of the parties, we have concluded that the arbitrary preference established in favor of males by 15–314 of the Idaho Code cannot stand in the face of the Fourteenth Amendment's command that no State deny the equal protection of the laws to any person within its jurisdiction. Idaho does not, of course, deny letters of administration to women altogether. Indeed, under

15–312, a woman whose spouse dies intestate has a preference over a son, father, brother, or any other male relative of the decedent. Moreover, we can judicially notice that in this country, a large proportion of estates, both intestate and under wills of decedents, are administered by surviving widows. Section 15–314 is restricted in its operation to those situations where competing applications for letters of administration have been filed by both male and female members of the same entitlement class established by 15–312. In such situations, 15–314 provides that different treatment be accorded to the applicants on the basis of their sex; it thus establishes a classification subject to scrutiny under the Equal Protection Clause. In applying that clause, this Court has consistently recognized that the Fourteenth Amendment does not deny to States the power to treat different classes of persons in different ways. The Equal Protection Clause of that amendment does, however, deny to States the power to legislate that different treatment be accorded to persons placed by a statute into different classes on the basis of criteria wholly unrelated to the objective of that statute. A classification "must be reasonable, not arbitrary, and must rest upon some ground of difference having a fair and substantial relation to the object of the legislation, so that all persons similarly circumstanced shall be treated alike." *Royster Guano Co. v. Virginia. (1920).*

The question presented by this case, then, is whether a difference in the sex of competing applicants for letters of administration bears a rational relationship to a state objective that is sought to be advanced by the operation of 15–312 and 15–314. In upholding the latter section, the Idaho Supreme Court concluded that its objective was to eliminate one area of controversy when two or more persons, equally entitled under 15–312, seek letters of administration and thereby present the probate court "with the issue of which one should be named." The court also concluded that where such persons are not of the same sex, the elimination of females from consideration "is neither illogical nor arbitrary method devised by the legislature to resolve an issue that would otherwise require a hearing as to the relative merits … of the two or more petitioning relatives. Clearly the objective of reducing the workload on probate courts by eliminating one class of contests is not without some legitimacy. The crucial question, however, is whether 15–314 advances that objective in a manner consistent with the command of the Equal Protection Clause. We hold that it does not. To give a mandatory preference to members of either sex over members of the other, merely to accomplish the elimination of hearings on the merits, is to make the very kind of arbitrary legislative choice forbidden by the Equal Protection Clause of the Fourteenth Amendment; and whatever may be said to the positive values of avoiding intrafamily controversy, the choice in this context may not lawfully be mandated solely on the basis of sex. We noted finally that if 15–314 is viewed merely as a modifying appendage to 15–312 and as aimed at the same objective, its constitutionality is not thereby saved. The objective of 15–312 clearly is to establish degrees of entitlement of various classes of persons in accordance with their varying degrees and kinds of relationship to the intestate. Regardless of their sex, persons within any one of the enumerated classes of that section are similarly situated with respect to that objective. By providing dissimilar treatment for men and women who are thus similarly situated, the challenged section violates the Equal Protection Clause. The judgment of the

Idaho Supreme Court is reversed and the case remanded for further proceedings not inconsistent with this opinion.

Text 4: Roe v. Wade, 410 U.S. 113 (1973)
Majority opinion of the court delivered by Justice Blackmun (excerpt)

The Constitution does not explicitly mention any right of privacy. In a line of decisions, however, going back perhaps as far as *Union Pacific R.Co. v. Botsford.* (1891), the Court has recognized that a right of personal privacy, or a guarantee of certain areas or zones of privacy, does exist under the Constitution. In varying contexts the Court or individual justices have indeed found at least the roots of that right in the First Amendment, in the Fourth and Fifth Amendments, in the penumbras of the Bill of Rights, in the Ninth Amendment ... or in the concept of liberty guaranteed by the first section of the Fourteenth Amendment. This right of privacy, whether it be founded in the Fourteenth Amendment's concept of personal liberty and restrictions upon state action, as we feel it is, or, as the District Court determined, in the Ninth Amendment's reservation of rights to the people, is broad enough to encompass a woman's decision whether or not to terminate her pregnancy. The detriment that the State would impose upon the pregnant woman by denying this choice altogether is apparent. Specific and direct harm medically diagnosable even in early pregnancy may be involved. Maternity, or additional offspring, may force upon the woman a distressful life and future. Psychological harm may be imminent. Mental and physical health may be taxed by child care. There is also the distress, for all concerned, associated with the unwanted child, and there is the problem of bringing a child into a family already unable, psychologically and otherwise, to care for it. In other cases, as in this one, the additional difficulties and continuing stigma of unwed motherhood may be involved. All these are factors the woman and her responsible physician necessarily will consider in consultation. On the basis of elements such as these, appellants and some amici argue that the woman's right is absolute and that she is entitled to terminate her pregnancy at whatever time, in whatever way, and for whatever reason she alone chooses. With this we do not agree. Appellants' arguments that Texas either has no valid interest at all in regulating the abortion decision, or no interest strong enough to support any limitation upon the woman's sole determination, [are] unpersuasive. The Court's decisions recognizing a right of privacy also acknowledge that some state regulation in areas protected by that right is appropriate. As noted above, a state may properly assert important interests in safeguarding health, in maintaining medical standards, and in protecting potential life. At some point in pregnancy, these respective interests become sufficiently compelling to sustain regulation of the factors that govern the abortion decision. The privacy right involved, therefore, cannot be said to be absolute. Where certain "fundamental rights" are involved, the Court has held that regulation limiting these rights may be justified only by a "compelling state interest," and that legislative enactments must be narrowly drawn to express only the legitimate state interests at stake. The District Court held that the appellee failed to meet his burden of demonstrating that the Texas statute's infringement upon Roe's rights was necessary to support a compelling state interest, and that, although the [appellee] presented "several compelling justifications for state presence in the area of abortions," the statutes outstripped these justifications and swept "far beyond any areas of compelling state interest.". Appellant and appellee both contest that holding. The appellee and certain amici argue that the fetus is a "person" within the language and meaning of the Fourteenth Amendment. In support of this they outline at length and in detail the well-known facts of fetal development. If this suggestion of personhood is established, the appellant's case, of course, collapses, for the fetus' right to life [would] then [be] guaranteed specifically by the Amendment. The appellant conceded as much on reargument. On the other hand, the appellee conceded on rearguments that no case could be cited that holds that a fetus is a person within the meaning of the Fourteenth Amendment. The Constitution does not define "person". in so many words. Section 1 of the Fourteenth Amendment contains three references to "person." But in nearly all … instances, the use of the word is such that it has application only postnatally. None indicates, with any assurance, that it has any possible pre-natal application. All this, together with our observation, supra, that throughout the major portion of the 19th century prevailing legal abortion practices were far freer than they are today, persuades us that the word "person," as used in the Fourteenth Amendment, does not include the unborn. This is in accord with the results reached in those few cases where the issue has been squarely presented. The pregnant woman cannot be isolated in her privacy. She carries an embryo and, later, a fetus, if one accepts the medical definitions of the developing young in the human uterus. The situation therefore is inherently different from marital intimacy, or bedroom possession of obscene material, or marriage, or procreation, or education, with which *Eisenstadt*, and *Griswold*, *Stanley*, *Loving*, *Skinner*, *Pierce*, and *Meyer* were respectively concerned. As we have intimated above, it is reasonable and appropriate for a State to decide that at some point in time another interest, that of health of the mother or that of potential human life, becomes significantly involved. The woman's privacy is no longer sole and any right of privacy she possesses must be measured accordingly. Texas urges that, apart from the Fourteenth Amendment, life begins at conception and is present throughout pregnancy, and that, therefore, the State has a compelling interest in protecting that life from and after conception. We need not resolve the difficult question of when life begins. When those trained in the respective disciplines of medicine, philosophy, and theology are unable to arrive at any consensus, the judiciary, at this point in the development of man's knowledge, is not in a position to speculate as to the answer. In view of all this, we do not agree that, by adopting one theory of life, Texas may override the rights of the pregnant woman that are at stake. We repeat, however, that the State does have an important and legitimate interest in preserving and protecting the health of the pregnant woman, whether she be a resident of the State or a nonresident who seeks medical consultation and treatment there, and that it has still another important and legitimate interest in protecting the potentiality of human life. These interests are separate and distinct. Each grows in substantiality as the woman approaches term and, at a point during pregnancy, each becomes "compelling." With respect to the State's important and legitimate interest in the health of the mother, the "compelling point, in the light of present medical knowledge, is at approximately the end of the first trimester. This is so because of the now established medical fact that until the end of the first trimester mortality in abortion may be less than mortality in normal childbirth. It follows that, from and after this point, a State may regulate the abortion procedure to the extent that the regulation reasonably relates to the preservation and protection of maternal health. This means, on the other hand, that, for the period of pregnancy prior to this "compelling" point, the attending physician, in consultation with his patient, is free to determine, without regulation by the State, that, in his medical judgment the patient's pregnancy should be terminated. If that decision is reached, the judgment may be effectuated by an abortion free of interference by the State. With respect to the State's important and legitimate interest in potential life, the "compelling" point is at viability. This is so because the fetus then presumably has the capability of meaningful life outside the mother's womb. State regulation protective of fetal life after viability thus has both logical and biological justifications. If the State is interested in protecting fetal life after viability, it may go so far as to proscribe abortion during that period, except when it is necessary to preserve the life or health of the mother. Measured against these standards, Art.1196 of the Texas Penal Code, in restricting legal abortions to those "procured or attempted by medical advice for the purpose of saving the life of the mother," sweeps too broadly. The statute makes no distinction between abortions performed early in pregnancy and those performed later, and it limits to a single reason, "saving" the mother's life, the legal justification for the procedure. The statute, therefore, cannot survive the constitutional attack made upon it here.

Index

In the series DISCOURSE APPROACHES TO POLITICS, SOCIETY AND CULTURE (DAPSAC) the following titles have been published thus far or are scheduled for publication:

1. GELBER, Katharine: *Speaking Back: The free speech versus hate speech debate.* 2002.
2. LITOSSELITI, Lia and Jane SUNDERLAND (eds.): *Gender Identity and Discourse Analysis.* 2002.
3. CHNG, Huang Hoon: *Separate and Unequal. Judicial rhetoric and women's rights.* 2002.
4. CHILTON, Paul and Christina SCHÄFFNER (eds.): *Politics as Talk and Text: Analytic approaches to political discourse.* n.y.p.